Watering Hole:

A User's Guide to Montana Bars

Introduction to the Second Printing

I read "Watering Hole" last night for the first time since it was published in 1980. Needless to say, it brought back some memories.

Now the book is to be reprinted, says the publisher, and there is no time for a full update. So these few paragraphs will have to suffice.

There is no way I can know how many of the bars still function, how many of the bartenders featured are still behind the plank. But I do know of a few changes and I will relate them here.

Charley Judd of Butte's New Deal died in the spring of 1981. His son, a Maryknoll priest, spoke at the funeral. At the end of an emotional remembrance that left few eyes in the packed church dry, he invited everyone to the New Deal for a post funeral wake. All drinks were free for the rest of the day and friends brought various dishes for a large potluck. Another New Deal party. Charley would have loved it.

The Wyokies are no longer playing at the Helsinki, as far as I know. The cost for use of the steamroom has gone up slightly, but it's still more than worth the cost.

The Rialto in Helena is still there, but probably wouldn't be featured if I were to do the book today. I heard the Bale of Hay Saloon in Virginia City burned down a year or so ago. That was a real loss to the state, as well as the nation—one of the most authentic saloons to be found anywhere. My first thought on hearing it burned was that I hoped they saved the moving picture nickolodians.

According to reports, Bob Gohn, the blind bartender who runs Bob's Place, is still there. It's worth a trip to Virginia City to see him.

The Top Hat in Missoula continues its decadent ways. I assume the Missoula Club still tosses its famous burgers.

The Dirty Shame in the Yaak is still there. Where would it go? I assume Sonny O'Day is still in Laurel. I hope so. I tried to call Luigi's in Butte the other night, but there was no number listed. I hope that doesn't mean what it would appear to mean.

But nothing lasts forever, not the Fun House of Entertainment, nor a paperback book on Montana bars. But after all, as mentioned in the explanation for this book, its purpose is only to chronicle one point in a continuum. I did my search. Everybody who reads this has a search of their own. Luckily, in Montana, the hunt rarely goes without many choice finds. Cheers.

Joan Melcher
October, 1983

Watering Hole:
A User's Guide to Montana Bars

by Joan Melcher

Illustrations by Nik Carpenter

Montana Magazine, Incorporated
Helena, Montana 1980

Second Printing, 1983

Published by Montana Magazine, Inc.
Box 5630 ● Helena, Montana 59601
Publisher — Rick Graetz
Editor — Mark Thompson
Assistant Editor — Carolyn Cunningham

ISBN 0-938314-00-9

To the bartenders.

Acknowledgements

Thanks to the many people who accompanied me on my search, notably Gail Seccomb, Steve Hinick, Barbara and Charlie Bennetts, Kate Heffern, Chris Mangiantini, Shephard Sherbell, and Hannah Thompson.
And to
Dave Walters, for his persistent assistance at the Montana Historical Society Library
Artist Nik Carpenter, who illustrated in two months what it had taken me two years to write
Historian and author K. Ross Toole for encouragement and suggestions offered
The Smith Gang, whose habit of barhopping across Montana did much to inspire my search.

Table of Contents

Foreword

It is rather astonishing that an institution as important
as the western bar should have almost entirely escaped
the attention of historians. It may be that historians have
simply made the a priori judgment that people went to
bars merely to carouse and shoot each other.

More probably the subject has been largely ignored
because the material for research simply isn't there — or
is so sparse as to render serious study almost impossible.
Saloon owners and bartenders were not record keepers.
There was no IRS around and these men, by their very
nature, were not given to accounts and ledgers.

It is true that one can glean enticing morsels from the
newspapers of the 1860s, '70s, and '80s. But morsels are
not substance. Except that, reading between the lines,
one gets the "inkling" that the early western saloon was
a social club, a place where very serious business was
done, a place used as frequently by the pillars of the
community as by road agents and riffraff. In places like
Butte and Red Lodge it had strong ethnic colorations. The
Irish had their places, the Finns theirs, the Italians theirs.

Historians are constantly adjured not to "read the
present into the past." But like all academic adjurations
this one should be taken with a generous measure of
salt. Clearly there is a world of difference between
today's "cocktail lounge" and today's "bar" or "saloon."
Bernard De Voto found even the "cocktail lounge" worthy
of a sprightly study, The Cocktail Hour. But he did not
concern himself with the saloon.

When Joan Melcher first started research on this book,
her intent was to produce a comprehensive historical
study of the western saloon. She asked me for
suggestions, but though I greeted the project with great
enthusiasm, I really couldn't help her except to suggest
that, though the enterprise was manifestly worthy, it was
equally perilous. She came to the same conclusion and
for awhile I thought the project was regrettably dead. In
fact, however, it was not and this book is the result.

If you thumb through this book cursorily you will
conclude that it is a commentary on today's saloons in
various Montana cities — saloons both old and new, west
and east — that it is a well written, humorous, and

sympathetic treatment. In a way it is a kind of guide to Montana's most interesting saloons. And it makes you want to visit them and see for yourself.

But if you sit down and give this book a little solid attention you will find that it is a great deal more than a once-over-lightly guide book. Joan Melcher has subtly ignored the rule "do not read today into yesterday." She has done this with profit to history and with skill and sensitivity. It is clear that in certain basic respects the role of the western saloon remains what it has always been. As an institution of importance it has always had its detractors — indeed it has always been venomously attacked by the pious and the righteous. The attacks have never really mattered to the keepers of the institutions nor to the patrons. The western saloon is simply too important a social, economic, and political instrument of western society to be turned aside from its predestined course. This is an intriguing, funny, and, mark you, an important book.

K. Ross Toole
Hammond Professor of
Western History
University of Montana

How It All Began:

A Select History of the Montana Saloon

Montana's first bar probably was no more than a plank of wood laid across two whiskey kegs. It might have been set up on a mountain pass by a prospector who used his grubstake to buy a supply of whiskey to sell to weary travelers. Or perhaps it was the first counter top of an enterprising merchant who brought a stock from the East to sell to trappers in the Northwest Territory. The first bartender may have been an itinerant whose purpose was to raise enough money to get to the next gold strike. Or he may have been a hard-working young man who would later achieve wealth and community stature. He may even have been a she, although the small percentage of women in Montana in those early days makes that unlikely.

One thing we know for certain. The famed plank was here shortly after men were. Eventually, the plank and kegs were covered by a tent. Tacked on the front of the canvas often was a hand-lettered sign heralding what lay within. Historic photographs show tent saloons in several Montana towns, often with a proud proprietor posing outside.

The tent saloon was crude and makeshift in comparison to the elaborate saloons that were to proliferate in the latter part of the 19th century. But there were few solid structures of any sort in early day Montana. A tent was a luxury to men who rarely slept with anything but stars overhead. Often the tent saloon was the main mercantile in town. And when optimism in the cowtowns and mining camps reached a fevered pitch and men began erecting solid structures, the saloon was among the first.

Back bars and accompanying saloon fixtures were sent from points East up the Missouri by steamboat to Fort Benton. Beginning in the 1860s this inland waterway was to play a key role in the settlement of Montana and an even more important role in the territory's social life. It opened the door to an era of shining mahogany, gleaming mirrors, brass foot rails and the veiled ladies in gilded frames.

The Social Sanctuary

Montana was settled by single men — adventurers, drifters, opportunists, fugitives from the law. Many had left comfortable livelihoods in the East on the gamble of untold wealth. Others were compulsive drifters whose glance invariably turned to greener pastures. Some were young romantics; others, no doubt, lawless misfits. Many were veterans of the Civil War — Confederate as well as Union soldiers — who carried their enmity to new ground. Many had come to Montana by way of gold or silver camps in Arizona, Nevada, Colorado, New Mexico.

These men met with a more beautiful, yet hostile nature than they probably had ever known, often going for days or weeks without seeing another human being. The mining camps and trail heads, as tenuous as they were, offered as much "civilization" as they were to find.

They must have been, at times, lonely, depressed, afraid, smitten with severe cases of cabin fever. For all the obvious reasons, they needed to drink. But there were countless other reasons they frequented the saloon.

In the absence of any other gathering spot, the saloon was town hall, church, livery stable, hotel, cafe, theatre, reading room, election hall, stage stop and bank. Wakes, weddings, funerals and baptisms were held in the saloon. Wandering minstrels found a ready stage there. Accommodating bartenders held a miner's poke and were trusted more than the bankers who were to arrive much later. Newcomers to the camp were allowed to sleep on the floor of a saloon until other accommodations were available. Elections were held there, as well as inspiring church services. Major community decisions were made there, as well as business transactions that were to affect a territory the size of four eastern states. Later journalists would be given expense accounts for the saloon, considered a prime source for news leads. And regardless of what they tell you, there was such a thing as a free lunch — in the early day saloon.

That plank of wood laid across kegs was to become the social sanctuary of the West.

All the Major Decisions . . .

The decision to apply for territorial status for Montana was reached by a group of Montana pioneers passing a Sunday afternoon in a Bannack saloon, according to one account. Reportedly John Con Orem, famed pugilist, blacksmith and saloon owner, was among the group, as well as Sidney Edgerton, who was to be named the first territorial governor.

The distance of Lewiston (Idaho), then capital of the territory, was a sore point among Montana settlers. Orem, in one of his many Sunday afternoon oratories in this particular saloon, called for seeking territorial status. Soon after, petitions were circulated among the mining camps and a collection of gold dust taken to pay Edgerton's way to Washington. The news came of Edgerton's success:

> Much gold was pinched from pokes in Bannack
> saloons that night. Everyone felt they were making
> history, as they were for that matter. Bannack, the
> glory of which was beginning to wane on account of
> strikes that were being made in Alder Gulch and
> elsewhere, took on a new lease on life . . . . Then
> Virginia City, much larger than Bannack, decided
> that she wanted the capitol, and took it . . . . More
> gold dust was pinched from gold pokes in the
> saloons of Bannack that night by way of
> consolation[1].

Bannack was not only to lose the capital but also her favorite son, to a booming Virginia City. Con Orem was to establish the Champion Saloon in Virginia City, where he easily combined his pugilistic career with saloon life. Advertisements that appeared in the *Montana Post* in 1864 hailed Orem's saloon as "adorned with the best set of sporting pictures west of New York," and added: "Private Lessons in boxing and sparring once a week."

Fights and Fights about Fights . . .

Sporting events were promoted heavily through the saloon, and Orem was to figure in many of the noteworthy promotions of early day Montana. A fighting hero to the

1. Montana News Association Inserts, July 1918, Montana Historical Society.

miners of the camp, Orem occasionally came out from behind the bar to meet a challenger. One fight was to go down in history. It matched Orem with Irishman Hugh O'Neil, who had both youth and 50 pounds on his side. Interest reached such intensity in Virginia City that the promoter of the fight erected a boxing arena in a log building behind Orem's saloon.

Orem and O'Neil fought 185 rounds, from evening until dawn, when the referee finally called the match a draw.

Another fight was to last even longer. One historian writes of a running fight about a fight:

> Perhaps the most famous drinking argument in history is one that raged in American saloons for nearly three-quarters of a century. That basic dispute concerns whether Custer and his troops were drunk the night before their battle. Many Indians claimed they were — that was why the Indians decided to fight. A man espoused the 'drunk' theory in a saloon in Helena one night. Another patron accused the man of mental clumsiness, then called him a known thief of soiled garments of blind laundry girls and the fight was on . . .[2]

The writer went on to say, "the question became extremely sensitive in Montana, and concluded: "Some people said more people were killed in arguments than were slain in the battle."

Then there were the fights of a more spontaneous nature:

> When Forsyth, Montana, was the end of the line on the Northern Pacific, 12 saloons arrived in sections, each with the conventional bar, beer cooler, table and piano. 'The bartender' in one joint was setting out the drinks before the roof was on, the professor was spanking the ivories, and in a matter of hours a man had already been shot in an argument over a dance hall girl.[3]

Fights and killings were clearly part of the early Montana saloon. But even the most celebrated of male bastions had its domestic side. A sign in an early Helena saloon admonished: "Don't Forget to Write dear Mother. She is thinking of you. We furnish paper and envelopes free and have the best whiskey in town."

The Saturday Night Bath

Saloons offering bath houses for their clientele probably contributed greatly to the tradition of the Saturday night

2. Robert L. Brown, "Saloons of the American West," *Denver Westerners' Roundup*, Vol. 29, March-April, 1973.
3. Brown, "Saloons of the American West."

Tent bar in Glasgow, Montana, 1880s.
Photo Courtesy of Montana Historical Society

bath. A miner of early day Emery, Montana, gives us a look at one such bath. In his reminiscenses of life in Emery, Bob Powell describes one of the town's favorite characters and the night the man met his nemesis:

> Billy didn't cut his hair nor did he trim his beard. He had an aversion to water so he didn't wash Billy and he didn't wash Billy's clothes. He claimed if he cut his hair, he'd bleed to death and if he used soap he'd break out in a rash . . . . Bill disliked soap and water but never did turn down whiskey. He went to Deer Lodge one time and a bunch of the boys got him drunk. Then they put him in a bath tub and soaked and scrubbed until they got him a complete new outfit of clothes and had his picture taken, too. To everyone's surprise he was one of the finest looking men you ever saw. He photographed so well that the picture was on display for months.[4]

Bartenders, Vagrants, and Celebrities . . .

The bartenders of the early days were often some of the best-liked and most respected citizens of the community. An early settler, Samuel William Carvoso Whipps, gives testimony to the good-heartedness of a couple of early Montana bartenders in the March 25, 1867, entry to his diary. Whipps had lived in various towns in Montana before this day, which found him in Livingston:

> One day I stepped into a saloon to get a bottle of whiskey. Much to my surprise this place was run by my old friend of Sidney days, Joe Lane, who ran the dance hall. He, his woman old Em, and Calamity Jane were there. Had I been their long lost son they could not have been gladder to see me. All of these people of the class usually condemned by preachers were big-hearted, generous people. Calamity Jane was noted for her kindness and generosity to the down and outs. She would divide her last crumb with them. A peculiar woman, generally wearing men's clothing, she was a noted and successful gambler and quick on the trigger, like poor old Jerry Phillips, who ran the most notorious place ever in Kalispell . . . . Both helped with money and fed thousands of down and outs.[5]

The saloon did attract its share of vagrants. But, it was one of a few, if not the only, public structure in a camp. It provided most of the basic services, including the most basic — shelter from the cold and the heat.

4. Bob Powell Reminiscenses, Montana Historical Society.
5. Samuel William Carvoso Whipps Diary, Montana Historical Society.

Bartenders' methods of dealing with loafers varied widely, and met with varying degrees of success. A newspaper story that appeared in *The New Northwest*, a Deer Lodge paper, in February of 1879, detailed the trouble one bartender had with dislodging a loafer from the saloon's coal stove. The story noted that the loafer had declined politely twice when asked if he would like to buy a hot drink, and took out his pipe when asked if he'd like to indulge in a fine cigar.

The bartender had placed a ball and cartridge on the stove for just this occasion. He walked to the stove; then leaped back from it, claiming the cartridge was about to go off. When asked when the thing would fire, the bartender shouted to the vagrant: "You haven't a minute to live if you don't get outdoors . . ." But the bartender had picked the wrong vagrant:

'Peter Adams,' began the stranger, as he shook off his old overcoat, 'you hain't got a tarnal thing to live for, and you might as well go under now, when coffins are cheap. Brace up, old boy, and die with your boots on — whoop!'

Picking up a stool he knocked the hot water can off the stove at the first blow and he was whaling away at the beer tables when the saloonist rushed in and screamed out:

'Fly! Fly! or you're a dead man!'

'Welcome, king of terrors,' whooped Peter as he tossed a table clear over the barkeep's head.

Three or four men came in to help secure him, but before they had succeeded jamming him down behind the coal box they had bumps and bruises to last them a month . . . .

But if bartenders had to contend with vagrants and trouble makers, they also rubbed elbows with some of the more successful men of their time. One saloon in Butte — the Orpheum — was known to host the big name performers who played in Butte during the town's heyday. Pictures of celebrities crowded the walls of the Orpheum, wrote a Butte journalist in 1919, adding that visiting celebrities would stop by "to see if their picture was still on the wall or donate one to the collection."[6]

The journalist talked of one of the more celebrated of Orpheum patrons: "Chaplin pretty nearly lived in the place the week he was in the vaudeville play *A Night in a London Music Hall* . . . We put on many a show that was better than the one you saw on the stage . . . ."

6. Byron Cooney, "The Saloons of Yesteryear," *The Montana American*, July 18, 1919.

The Free Lunch

And for all the men — Peter Adamses as well as Charlie Chaplins — there was the free lunch. Used primarily as an enticement to drink, the free lunch came to be the main sustenance of many. Old timers remember how the free lunch carried them through lean times. A Miles City bartender, Charlie Brown, was known to keep a pot of mulligan stew on the stove 24 hours a day for hungry customers.[7]

But it was in Butte that the free lunch reached its full potential. An article in the January 4, 1892 *Montana Standard* first chastised the vagrants who took advantage of the free lunch and then went on to describe, in mouth-watering detail, the delicacies offered. The headline of the story declared: *How Hundreds of Lazy Men Secure a Free Meal;* a subhead reiterated: *Bums and Vags Who Believe That the World Owes Them a Living — What They Eat.*

The story described the free lunch circuit in Butte: "There are half a dozen saloons in the city each of which gets up more things to eat free than the two best hotels in Butte at any price." The reporter obviously had indulged, himself. He listed off several saloons and the bills of fare for which they were famous, including lobster, roast pig, imported sausages, sardines, herrings and oysters on the half shell.

The saloon, like an old, but spry vaudevillian with a trunk full of masks, was to change its identity constantly. When it wasn't serving some of the best food in town, it was hosting a prize fight, counting ballots from a camp election or baptizing a baby.

A Wake . . .

The saloon's role as church is one of its most interesting incarnations. Weddings, funerals, baptisms — all were performed in the saloon, to say nothing of weekly services. One historian claims bartenders encouraged preachers to hold services in their establishments because their customers' enthusiasm in worship was quickly converted to enthusiasm for the bottle.[8]

But one story of a wake held in an early day Montana saloon shows how some men needed no encouragement. The story, told by pioneer Henry Bose, begins with the death of Irishman Micky at Last Chance Gulch. Micky made his friends promise to bury him in consecrated ground, with a priest attending. Bose explains that the nearest priest at that time was in Deer Lodge, so a group of men made a coffin and formed a large procession for Deer Lodge, headed up by a

7. Richard Erdoes, *Saloons of the Old West*, Alfred A. Knopf, Inc., New York, 1979.
8. Elliot West, *The Saloon on the Rocky Mountain Mining Frontier*, University of Nebraska Press, Lincoln and London, 1979.

wagon carrying the body:

> At Pioneer bar there was some ground sluice and we found there was a saloon. As it was late in the afternoon some of the boys went in and had a drink, and pretty soon they went in and had another drink. Then we concluded that poor Micky had never had a wake and we should bring him in and hold a real Irish wake. We got some candles and brought the coffin in and sat it on two beer kegs. We took off the lid and lighted the candles and there was poor Micky layin' in there. We had some real good singing and drinking all night. The boys all got pretty tired — so we made our beds on the floor around the coffin . . . ."

The next day the group set out for Deer Lodge. Bose and another rode ahead to make preparations with the priest for burial, but when the procession arrived in Deer Lodge, there was no coffin in the wagon. One of the men remembered the horses rearing at a river crossing, but it was too late to make the trip back. Bose remembers:

> We all went to Deer Lodge and had a meeting in Pete Valiton's Brewery. The next morning Jim and I and two more started out from Deer Lodge in the wagon. At the top of the hill we found the place where the horses had acted up and after a long search we found the coffin in the creek bed where it rolled. And there was poor Micky standing on his head. We had an awful time getting the water out of the coffin, but we brought the body up to Deer Lodge and buried it reverently with proper ceremonies.[9]

The Falling Shadow of Prohibition

By the turn of the century the Montana saloon had become an institution. Over four decades it had grown increasingly more lively, diverse, decorative, and perhaps a trifle arrogant. It had a reputation.

The camps also had grown. Tenuous settlements had become bustling trade centers. Town halls, hotels, mercantiles and churches had stripped the saloon of many of the roles it had once enjoyed. Montana towns finally were achieving some sort of permanence, and with that came the yearnings of a good part of the population to turn a camp into a community.

That longing for stability and community was to play straight into the hands of the Temperance Movement. The movement was gaining momentum in the East and making tentative inroads in the West.

9. Henry Bose Reminiscenses, Montana Historical Society.

But Montana was still skeptical. A news dispatch carried in the Butte Evening News in November 1907 cited Montana as "the only state 'Entirely Wet.'" The story credited Nevada and Idaho as competitors, but concluded that Montana was the only state where bars were open 24 hours a day.

The article may have sobered up a few Montanans. The next year was to see the passage of several city ordinances ordering the closure of saloons for a few hours every night. Several cities, including Helena, Missoula and Bozeman, passed what were called early closing ordinances. Most of the town newspapers editorialized against the ordinances, and often they passed by slim margins. Helena had a particularly lively session, but those for a more stable community were the winners. They claimed they could make Helena the educational center of the Northwest — one of the most progressive cities in the state as well as the nation — if the ordinance passed.[10]

In 1917 and 1918, as more and more states ratified the 18th Amendment to the Constitution, articles began to appear in newspapers, speculating on what the future might hold. The long-time rivalry between the smelter city and the richest hill on earth surfaced in one newspaper article. The Anaconda Standard ran a story on approaching Prohibition January 14, 1917. The headline was vindictive: *When the Saloon Door No Longer Swings To And Fro; When Beer No More Shall Flow, And The Whiskey Bottle Vanishes And All Other Wet Goods of Commerce Disappear And Butte Wakes Up To Find Herself Dry As A Bone.*

Predictably, in this working man's town, the lead of the story was the number of jobs that would be lost to Prohibition: "The total number of persons affected by the move, as near as can be figured from families of saloon workers, will be about 1,400."

Two years later, the amendment ratified, Byron E. Cooney, one of several talented Butte journalists of his age, wrote a lengthy tribute to Butte saloons. Years later, another Butte journalist was to write an epic poem to pre-Prohibition Butte bars. Through the 108 stanzas of "The Saloons of Old Time Butte," Bill Burke named and described some 233 bars.

Cooney's article took the reader on an entertaining, emotional tour of several classic Butte joints. Many of the old-time bartenders were closing their doors never to open them again. But a few were to remain open through more than 13 dry years.

Walker's in Butte was one of the survivors. Mr. Parker, the proprietor of Walker's, then a popular working man's bar,

10. *Helena Independent,* November 30, 1907.

claimed his near-beers were selling well and he planned to stay open. "Near-beer served ice cold is a palatable and healthful drink," Cooney quoted Parker.[11]

Walker's and countless old-time saloons like it were to become the speak-easies, the Hire's rootbeer outlets, the milkshake fountains and the card rooms. It was at this time that many of the old time saloons began stocking sporting goods and magazines. Prohibition did not kill the saloon. It just gave it one more role.

Montana and Prohibition

Of course, Montana was never truly dry. The state legislature had ratified the 18th Amendment to the Constitution in a special session in 1918, but in 1926 Montanans voted to repeal all state prohibition laws, leaving enforcement to the federal government. Having voted against it in a state ballot, Montanans seemed to prefer to believe Prohibition did not pertain to them.

The popular theory that people drank more during Prohibition than before or after, clearly holds water here. An article in a Butte newspaper during the period claimed 500 speak-easies. Traffic was also heavy in border towns. Before Prohibition, Canadians crossed the border for American whiskey. Now the shoe was on the other foot. Montana News Association articles later were to describe a moonshiner's relay from Canada, through Havre, to Denver and Salt Lake, and shorter runs between Canada and Montana:

> In every hotel along the High Line there are groups
> of men garbed like Arctic explorers ready to make a
> dash for the line. Their talk is not of the defeat of the
> Non-Partisan League, or the drop in the price of
> wheat, in both of which subjects there might be
> some local interest, but rather of the run they have
> made that day . . . .

Moonshine stills sprang up across the state, but there was an easier way to secure one's Mornin's Mornin'. Alcohol was sold under various guises across the drug store counter.

Moonshining and bootlegging were the subject of many articles that were to appear in Montana during Prohibition and after. An article in a Butte newspaper listed several alibis given by moonshiners: as a stimulant for a baby; for money to feed children; a preparation for cleaning clothes; as a liniment, and for bathing.

Other articles warned the customer to be wary of the "poteen." One cautioned that one in every 10 bootleggers were caught. A Missoula legislator made the mistake of claiming to

11. Cooney, "The Saloons of Yesteryear."

know of one bootlegging operation in 1919. The state's Attorney General subpoenaed him, but he claimed constitutional rights and was not made to testify.

But all that was to pass. The Noble Experiment was to be viewed as a miserable failure by 1932 and in 1933, the saloon doors were to swing open again. Only beer was to be legal for the first eight months. Moonshine whiskey had been available through much of Prohibition, but beer had been more difficult to obtain. Their breweries closed during Prohibition, Montanans awaited the arrival of beer from eastern breweries with great anticipation. One account notes that beer was legal April 7, 1933, but it could not be shipped before that day. It usually took four days to transport beer from the Minnesota brewery that was to supply Montana, but the writer noted, "somehow it got to Montana two days after it became legal . . . Hundreds walked or drove to the railroad stations; the supply was exhausted within a few hours."[12]

But, a look at Butte newspapers in early April tells another story. Several bars in Butte advertised a stock of eastern beers in the April 7 and 8 editions. Walker's had remained opened 24 hours every day through Prohibition. An advertisement in the Butte Daily Post claimed it had in stock the only draught beer in Montana. Walker's had survived more than 13 years of near-beer. It seemed only right.

12. Larry Quinn, Politicians in Business: *A History of the Liquor Control System in Montana*, University of Montana Press, 1970.

The Perfect Montana Bar

A Cold Spring Evening in West Glacier

One cold spring evening, a tiring day of travel behind me, I pull abruptly up to a bar on the outskirts of West Glacier, Montana. I need a bracer and a change of position after four days on the road.

The bar is beginning to fill with regulars. I sip my burgundy, as comfortable as I would be in my own kitchen, and watch happy hour in West Glacier.

Two couples are drinking beer, bantering with the bartender. No one speaks to me — I'm the audience — but I laugh along with the jokes. One of the women sits up on her stool to peer out the window, laughingly referring to "Old Tim."

The bartender whispers aside to me that the mayor of the town is coming. The door squeaks slowly open, letting in the damp of rain and cold, and Old Tim shuffles comfortably in, an old wool hat pulled tightly down over an old Irish head. He takes a stool near mine.

Every town should have an honorary mayor like Tim — wise, grizzled, not afraid to walk a few blocks in the spring rain to happy hour in his favorite bar, where with slight encouragement he will pass on to the younger folks a few insights into the mysteries of life.

Tim's maxim tonight, mumbled in a raspy broque, is "Ah, just keep a cool head and a dry back, and you'll be just fine."

The regulars and I agree it's not bad advice, and while they shoot pool, I contemplate my good fortune. Having stopped along the road at an unknown tavern, I have found laughter, wine to warm my insides and relax my stiffened limbs, companionship from people I can't call by name, and even a bit of country philosophy from an old Irishman who worked the mines in Butte.

I have found the Montana bar. And it's still functioning as the social sanctuary of the West.

It's still a place to buy supplies, fill up the gas tank, eat dinner, end a long night of good-timing. A place where life-long plans and promises are made; and just as quickly broken. A place to cry in your beer over life's inherent injustice — before you laugh with abandonment in the glow of one too many beers. A place to dance when the juke boxes' western twang becomes too melancholy or too exuberant for a body's rhythm to ignore.

More than anything, it's a place to gather. With five people to every square mile, Montana — as beautiful and accommodating as she can be — is still a lonely place, remote, a land of seemingly endless proportion that dwarfs people, frightens them, pulls them to one another. The town bar has always been the gathering place for the people who populated the harsh plains, the ominous mountains. Sometimes there was no town, but stuck out alone and brave, a refuge to the people tucked in the land's folds, was the Montana bar.

I would not try to gloss over the darker side of bar life — that well-earned reputation for sheltering degenerates, drunkeness, brawls, killings and marital disputes.

Still, consumption of alcohol is often an incidental factor in the Montana bar. When the whole range of human emotion and intellect is passed across the bar, down the stools, absorbed in the grains of wood through decades, generations, what import is there really to a few ditches, a few drafts, a few

Montana Bar in Miles City

boilermakers? As sacred as liquor is to many Montanans, it has little to do with why most of us frequent a favorite bar.

You might find the best cup of coffee you've had in weeks there; or a hot, brisk cup of tea. Often you can buy milk and eggs there, a steak dinner, a sandwich, a newspaper or a ticket to the next town event. You'll find pool tables, pinochle tournaments, bluegrass bands, honky tonk piano; stony silences in a river of talk; fist fights amid romance; friends, relatives, strangers.

And because I found companionship with strangers that cold spring night in a bar I'd never seen and might not venture across again; because I sensed in that bar a phenomenon that could explain the Montana character and way of life possibly better than any other single idea, I decided to go in search of the perfect Montana bar.

The Search Begins

That search began two years ago. Like a chef in search of the perfect souffle, a maestro in search of the perfect sonata, or the hard worker in search of the perfect Saturday night, I went in search of the perfect Montana bar.

I followed the Yellowstone east and the Clark Fork west. I went south to the Big Hole and north to the Yaak. The bravado of the Mission Mountains took my breath; the sweep of the plains gave it back. Sandstone ghosts met me in southeastern river valleys and pastel bluffs and buttes drew me along the Missouri. Virginia City held me for a weekend; the Yellowstone Valley for a week; Butte for months. The Highline was on my mind.

I made day trips, weekend trips, week-long trips. I racked up thousands of miles on my car. I took free-lance jobs so I'd be free to travel. When those began to dry up I took a full time job, squeezing out weekends and vacation time for more travel.

I took anyone who would go with me; more often I went alone. I found the bartenders were more likely to talk freely with me when I was alone. When I'd go with a man, they'd think I didn't want to be bothered. When I'd go with a woman, they'd leave us alone to talk. But when I was alone, the bartender became my host.

A solitary person nursing a draft beer is almost more than a good bartender can take. The bar's regulars had their own lives. The down-and-outers weren't feeling any pain. I was new to the place — and alone. Clearly I needed a friend. Time and again the bartenders took me in — telling me what they knew of their bar, introducing me to town characters, referring me to others.

There were times when I thought nothing was going right with my life. I'd jump in the Renault and head for another bar. There I would be greeted by yet another John Wayne of a bartender, with yet another story, another town character. I'd add another piece to a growing mosaic, and leave with a smile on my face.

I probably stopped in an eighth of the 1,600 bars in the state. I've written about less than half of those: the bad bars and the sad bars, gay bars and play bars; the stage stop bars, migrant bars, tourist bars, and bars for single cowboys; the mean bars and clean bars; the new bars, the rendition saloons, the old bootlegging joints.

I found bars with D-I-V-O-R-C-E written in the air, and bars that host community wedding dances. I found a woman trick roper and a delightfully mad puppeteer; Halloween parties for kids and pig roasts for the community. I found a boxing hall of fame in one bar and one of Montana's last sheepherders in another. I found milkshake fountains, shoeshine stands, Sen-Sen and sobriety; punchboards, poker, wino pits and prostitution.

I found that people like to leave a part of themselves in a bar. In Emigrant I found a saloon where customers toss coins over the back of the bar for good luck. In Reed Point travelers pound coins into a wood beam above the bar and then carve their names in the soft, smooth log. In Kalispell they tack a dollar above the bar so they will always have a drink coming. In Luigi's they leave a business card or a signed photograph.

Other patterns began to emerge. I found the best bars usually were those whose owners were gregarious and fair individuals who took an interest in the community; often they worked the day shift in their bar.

I found the most unique and true bars in the small towns, actually, the smaller the town the better. The small town bar is less influenced by the present — naturally tied to the past — or perhaps unlikely to draw a boundary between the two.

I found history living throughout my search. Butte's Orpheum lives in Luigi's Fun House of Entertainment; Con Orem's Champion Saloon in Sonny O'Day's boxing museum; Kalispell's compassionate Jerry Phillips in Moose Miller, and the spirit of Calamity Jane in Trixie's Antler Saloon. And I learned the free lunch still exists, indeed never died.

And just when I thought I had covered the state and it was time to retire both my car and my typewriter, friends began to point out bars I had missed. And I thought of others: the Radersburg bar, the Augusta bars at rodeo time, the roadhouses of the northwestern part of the state, Piszer's Palace in Butte. Time was marching on. The past and the present — history, legend, recent events — had blended in my search, leaving Time a confused participant. But it *had* run out.

People I hardly knew were asking me when the bar book was coming out. There was an abrupt awakening. Suddenly I knew I wasn't the only one who understood the elemental importance of the state's bars to the Montana psyche. I began to realize the responsibility I had shouldered when I purported to write a guide to Montana bars. Of 1,600 bars flung with abandon across the plains and the mountains, I had written about 50. I knew there were at least that many more out there deserving of equal attention.

But it was worse than that. It had gotten so my writing was interfering with my search. Did I ever find the perfect Montana bar? I'll leave you with this arm chair guide. When you're finished reading, I'll throw the reins your way.

Butte-Anaconda:
The Mother Lode

The M&M Cigar Store

9 North Main
Butte

The M&M is the dirty old man of Butte bars, a tobacco-stained grandfather who is still revered and respected for what he was in more vital days, and now, if for no other reason, because he's still around. Bartender Mickey Flynn tells me, "People who move away from Butte — they come back and want to locate friends. They come to the M&M."

The M&M always has been a bar of basics — good whiskey, good food, gambling styled to the inveterate gambler. It's been around for close to a century. The food's still as good, and not much more expensive than the early days. Drink prices have increased, but still are less than just about anywhere in the country, and there's at least as much gambling in the M&M as state law allows.

The M&M's front is unique in Montana — shiny steel in rich folds, a set of heavy steel doors below a large, mint green sign with arrows blinking to the bar's entrance. Inside is a long oak bar, stools lining it; directly across stands the cafe's equally-long counter, stools lining it. An art deco back bar, with lighted yellow columns, sits above well-kept oak cabinets.

At first glance the M&M appears to be an old man's bar, breathing, along with its patrons, a long, last breath. Yet there remains a feeling of action about the place. The back room, formerly one of Butte's key gambling joints, now hosts a serious keno game and day-long poker. A young woman works the keno cage with diligence, calling out the numbers over a microphone, her voice filling the bar and cafe counters in the front. Numbers and the rattle of keno balls echo in the M&M throughout the day and into the night.

Elderly women in stylish leisure suits — their faces heavily powdered, their lips apple red — sit on folding chairs in the back room and watch their keno cards. The M&M's plank is usually lined with old men, bent to the bar like old crows bent over a telephone wire. But the place still draws all kinds. A lunch hour at the M&M might find life insurance salesmen rubbing elbows with workers from the Berkeley Pit, Tony the Trader charming a legal secretary, a motorcycle bandit in deep conversation with an area rancher. The M&M is probably most interesting in the early morning hours after the bars have closed. One time I stopped in with friends about 3 a.m. and talked with a student of Chinese, who had been sitting for hours at the M&M cafe counter, drinking coffee, translating an ancient fable.

I've been in the M&M a few times for breakfast, either ending a day or beginning one. I remember one morning in particular. It was six and I was somewhat surprised to see old men enjoying their Mornin's Mornin' at the bar. I knew that Montana law forbids the sale of liquor from 2 to 8 a.m.

Today I ask Mickey Flynn about it. Mickey has tended bar in Butte for 46 years. He worked in the M&M early in his career and also ran his own bar for 18 years. The last eight years he's been back at the M&M. Mickey won't answer my question, but he shows me the hinges under the counter and the fronting that attaches. State people now insist the partition be put up between 2 and 8. Mickey's look is sly, but good-natured. He's learned to humor just about everyone, and he's seen a lot of changes in 46 years of bartending in Butte, but it seems this fronting over the bar is one of the more unusual things he's seen happen to the M&M.

The M&M probably has the largest regular clientele of any Butte bar, possibly any bar in the state. My favorite regular is an old Indian, a surprisingly good Western artist who sketches with a ballpoint pen on keno cards.

He drew for me one day when I stopped briefly to talk to him. His hands seemed to jump from corner to corner on the sheet, lines and curves coming from all over, but when he was finished, a clean, sharply drawn cowboy on a loping horse was there. I took it home, and later framed it — partly because it was quite good for a (ballpoint) pen and ink sketch, and partly because I was amazed at the quality considering the old man seemed quite drunk when he drew it.

Other men around the bar told me the artist — Walter Brown — was celebrated in some circles, had sold his art in younger days. It had been a few years since I had seen Walter, so I asked the M&M's new owner, Charlie Bugni, if he was still around. Oh yeah, he said, I think Wally went to Dillon today. Does he still draw? "Oh yeah, isn't it something. He can draw like that, and I can't even draw my breath."

The M&M still packs them in on days of celebration in Butte. In the face of years of decline in the Mining City, the M&M drew one of its largest crowds for St. Patrick's Day in 1978, and a larger one in 1979. The place was loaded — front to back — from morning through the night. In 1978 politicians running in the spring primary worked the crowd like they'd work a farmer's convention or a large church bazaar.

Charlie Bugni served corned beef and cabbage for a dollar a plate, complete with salad, mashed potatoes and coffee. On election day he serves an admirable steak, french fries, soup, salad, coffee and toast for two bucks. Of course, he can't break even with such deals, but Charlie operates the M&M in the Butte tradition: Good will and good deals keep the people coming in.

A small draft at the M&M is still twenty-five cents; a boilermaker (shot of whiskey, beer chaser) is a dollar. Mickey Flynn remembers when a boilermaker was ten cents. "When the men came off shift — anyone who carried a lunch bucket — we'd only charge them for the glass of beer — ten cents, a good 12-ounce one. The shot was free. Then the office workers and clerks wanted it, too. So they had to stop that."

The M&M was big time in Butte during the gambling years. The slot machines were in front; roulette, crap tables, 21 tables and Chinese lottery in the back.

"Everybody was here," the kind, respectable elderly Mickey tells me over a beer one afternoon. "All walks of life. It didn't make any difference. It was quite the place. The gambling hall ran 24 hours. They never locked the doors. During the war (WWII) they put the closing hours on. We had to go get locks and keys made."

"Shutdowns? Yeah we had shutdowns all the time, either before an election or after an election, depending on who was going to get the nomination."

Butte slipped through 13 years of Prohibition, her reputation as a drinking town nearly unscathed, thanks largely to places like the M&M where the upstairs did a healthy liquor trade. The downstairs covered as a restaurant and cigar store. Mickey said there was a peek hole in the door to the upstairs. "If you didn't like their looks you wouldn't let them in."

Busted during Prohibition? "Oh yeah. Stool pigeons from out of state came in and turned it (liquor) in. When it came time for the trial the evidence was disappeared — evaporated."

When Prohibition was lifted, hard liquor was still forbidden for a time, Mickey said. The bartenders at the M&M served the hard stuff, but kept the bottles out of sight. One day federal inspectors came in and Mickey was bartending. They hadn't expected the inspectors and a bottle was out. Mickey said he grabbed it and stood back up against the bar with the bottle between his legs. "I wore an apron then," he said. "They couldn't find it."

Mickey remembers when the feds would find a still or a liquor supply, take it out into the street and run it down the gutter. He remembers some men going out into the street to watch. "Some knelt down and got a drink. They just hated to see it go down the gutter."

Forty-six years behind the plank in Butte. What's it been like? "Lovely," Mickey says with his usual graciousness. "Better than four college educations. Everybody's troubles. I don't even know my own . . . ."

Luigi's
1826 Harrison Avenue
Butte
Closed Monday Nights

Luigi claims Neil Diamond wrote "A Beautiful Noise" about his bar. You'll be sitting at Luigi's on an ordinary night, and there will be a lapse in conversation or in the bizarre interaction between Luigi and his customers and Luigi's

eyebrows will jump, his malleable face will take on an excited-child expression, he'll point a long, straight arm to the juke box where Diamond's song is blaring, and stutter in his excitement to get the words out, "See, listen here now. It's a beautiful noise — the pipes you know, the pipes. And now listen — spiders and snakes. Neil Diamond wrote that song about this place. He was here one night."

"Beautiful Noise" could have been written about Luigi's, but it really doesn't matter. In my book, Luigi is bigger than Neil Diamond. As diverse and creative as the Montana bar can be, there is no bar in the world quite like Luigi's.

Luigi calls it a fun house of entertainment. Early in the evening it can be a visit to the circus or the theatre; a trip into fantasy or back into childhood. When Luigi *really* gets wound up, there is no better description for the place than a madhouse.

Luigi is a one-man band, a puppeteer, a clown, a mechanical wizard, a master of the one-liner, a comedian of dry, but sometimes wild wit, a showman extraordinaire. The man has systematically strung his bar for perpetual movement — light, music, puppets, all working in harmony, all part of a master electrical plan laid out by the mad genius himself.

The place actually jumps, spins, thumps, flashes, blinks, winks, groans and squeals with his creations: puppets of all shapes and sizes, snakes hanging from the ceiling, reptiles everywhere, some set up to routinely devour others, a monkey on a unicycle riding a tightrope, a hammer that drops to conk an unsuspecting customer when someone else opens the door, a full-sized mannequin that collapses when someone walks by, business cards and signed photos of famed personalities layered on the walls, a large gold fish Luigi has trained to swim through a hoop and kiss him when he puts his lips to the water; all tempered by circling colored lights that blink with a quiet amusement of their own.

"Everything that's done in here is original, you know," Luigi says. "See, we had psychedelic lights here first. Now the whole world's got 'em."

The main attraction, however, is still the world's largest one-man band, Luigi and his dancing dolls, all of which jump and gyrate to the carnival sound of Luigi on the accordian, drums, a couple of horns, a cymbal, water bottles, a xylophone and any object he can get his hands, feet or mouth to.

With the various instruments and Luigi's throaty voice as background, down from the ceiling come the spiders and snakes. Tiny creatures, perfectly formed. The spiders have 10 legs. The legs have joints. You can't see the hair-thin wires from the ceiling unless you look very close. A spotlight goes on the menagerie of reptiles and they dance to Luigi's insane beat, the spiders' legs and joints working naturally on the lighted tile, throwing large shadows across the empty dance floor.

Later in the night Luigi will find a regular or an energetic newcomer to mobilize the crowd. It's time to play the pipes. The pipes are old, hollowed out antennas in widely varying lengths. Luigi gets everyone in a circle and puts "A Beautiful Noise" on the juke box.

Soon people are down on their hands and knees — middle-aged women, a pair of traveling salesmen, teenagers, a couple in their early 30s, elderly pals of Luigi — they are down on their knees throwing pipes across the shiny linoleum at each other. People love it.

Nearly all Butte bars are great places to be on holidays and times for celebration. Like most of Butte, Luigi loves a good party — he throws one almost every night — but a holiday is cause for a better celebration.

I've spent a good part of several New Year's Eves in Luigi's. I remember best my first New Year's there. Every age group was represented. Luigi was wild with excitement as the clock ticked toward twelve. You would have thought it was his first New Year's. Old women danced together, one in a flowing gauze gown, a whimsical young girl's expression on her face. Luigi did the countdown and when he came to zero I thought the place would rise from the ground.

But let's look at a typical Luigi night. A middle-aged couple comes, unassuming, through the door and takes stools at the bar. Luigi serves them, and then bends down to monitor their conversation. He announces to the bar with appropriate hoopla — a child's glee in uncovering an adult wrong — "These two, right here. They're staying at the Ramada Inn, room 84, and they're not even marrrriiiiied."

The eyebrows shoot up dramatically. The mouth sets firmly into a prissy pucker. Luigi holds the expression like he's holding five gallons of water.

After several drinks, two traveling salesmen start toward the door. Luigi calls them to come back, promising, as he has for years, that a nurses' convention is in town. He moans and carries on about their leaving, but mumbles to those close to the bar, "There goes another five bucks."

A young construction worker comes out of the restroom. Luigi frantically points at the man proclaiming with the anxiety of a head nurse, "He didn't wash his hands."

As the night wears on, customers will be asking for a drink. Luigi usually says, "No thanks, I got one," or "Yes, I'll be with you in a half hour." When someone asks when Luigi is going to play, the answer usually is eight minutes. The truth is Luigi plays only when the feeling moves him. But he has played every night, six nights a week for 30 years. And every night he is On.

Asked if he tires of coming in every night and doing virtually the same thing, Luigi answers, "No. You know why? Cause people are beautiful."

So, the tremendous energy flows; the clown performs; the one-man band plays with wild exuberance; the bartender fixes drinks when he feels like it, and the one-liners emanate from Luigi like the flow of water on the downhill.

Luigi's first establishment was located in the Little Italy of Butte, called Meaderville, famous for its gambling, good food and uproarious nightlife. Meaderville was one of several neighborhoods swallowed by the Berkeley Pit.

When asked how he felt about moving from Meaderville, Luigi said, "Oh it was sad. Yeah, it was sooooo sad." Asked how long it took him to move his thousands of objects, he usually says, "Oh boy, about a case of vodka."

Helsinki Bar and Steambath

402 East Broadway
Butte

The Helsinki has live music Friday and Saturday night and Sunday afternoon. Ralph and Bill, two musicians who have seen a number of Friday and Saturday nights, call themselves the Wyokies. Their music is basic, straight-forward western pickin' on worn electric guitars.

One late night at the Helsinki the Wyokies were seated in their usual perch in the corner. It was a warm fall night and the front door was propped open. My friends and I heard a commotion outside. We looked toward the door in time to see an old man come in. The man's stomach leered out of sagging pants, but his carriage was upright and proud. At his mouth was an old bugle that he was blowing with the concentration of a Lawrence Welk soloist.

The bugle looked Civil War vintage, and the man wasn't much younger. He blew as he approached the bandstand, nearly falling over backward once when he took too much breath for a particular phrase. The surprising thing about it all was that the man was *good.* The Wyokies played their regular fare in constant 4/4 beat, paying little, if any, attention

to their colleague's counterpoint. The bugle player jumped around the melody, jazzing, jamming. Had the man been 20 years younger, sober, and with a presentable trumpet, we would have been in for some Music.

You can expect old men coming through the door blowing bugles at the Helsinki. The Helsinki is an extremely random sort of place — perhaps because it sits on the edge of that great abyss, the Berkeley Pit.

A crumbling East Broadway street ambles from Butte's uptown east to what appears to be the end of the road — the Helsinki, in white stucco framed in cheerful red and green neon lights. Standing alone, in direct defiance to the wall of mining waste across the street and the mile-wide open pit beyond, the Helsinki is the last holdout of Butte's once-thriving Finntown. It once was one of six bars on the block. In 1941 a few upstanding Finntown residents got up a petition to rescind the Helsinki's (then called the Corner Bar) license because there already were five saloons on the block and the Helsinki was a scant 300 feet from a church. Lucky for today's Finntown, the petition didn't fly. The five other saloons have succumbed to the pit, and the Helsinki, although quite lively some days and nights, has the demeanor of a place marked for death — a nonchalance bathed in fatalism.

The Helsinki has the oldest barmaid I've ever seen. Mary is a large, grey-haired, sprightly, competent woman who inspires a certain respect, notably from the many men she towers over. The night of the bugle player, Mary, not to be outdone, marched to the bandstand, took over the microphone, and sang — in a voice that once may have been melodious — a very old song. Regulars politely applauded.

The Helsinki isn't much to look at. Like nearly all Butte bars, though, the front and back bar are solid wood. Beautiful old oak cabinets with mirror backs hang on one wall. Their only contents are Helsinki-inscribed t-shirts. There's western art on the walls and a mountain sheep's head mounted, but all are covered with plastic, perhaps in an effort to save them from the dust emanating from the pit. An old photo, taken when the rest of Finntown stood around the Helsinki, hangs on the wall near the door.

On the back bar are tacked several signs: "Don't Stare at the Bartender — You May Be Goofy Yourself Someday," "We Understand Broken English Here," "Finn Power," and "Recreation Should Not Wreck Creation."

There is a definite feel of eastern Montana about the place. It could be because it stands out so alone; or because of the music; but I think it's probably more because of the cowboy boots. One realizes the influence of people from Scandinavia in eastern Montana when in the Helsinki. The Helsinki's Finnish clientele would fit comfortably in an eastern Montana cowboy bar. More cowboy boots per square foot can be found in the Helsinki on any given day than any other bar in Butte (excluding the El Mar).

The Helsinki serves as the axis for Butte's Finnish community. A proud and lively lot, Butte's Finns have resisted the melting pot by continuing a long tradition of playing and staying together: Picnics, celebrations of any kind, street dances on the crumbled pavement in front of the bar that last into early morning — Bacchus thumbing his nose at the ominous pit.

Not to be outdone by Butte's considerable Irish population, the Finns celebrate Saint Urho's Day the day before St. Patrick's day. Saint Patrick, the Irish claim, chased the snakes out of Ireland. Big deal, say the Finns, St. Urho chased the grasshoppers out of Finland and into Ireland. On March 16 — St. Urho's Day — so the legend goes — green-clad men kick like grasshoppers and turn from green to purple (the Finn's color).

The Helsinki's clientele are largely middle-aged to elderly Finns. They laugh and drink and dance and drink and cry in their beer and drink and dance some more. To many of them the Helsinki is home.

The Helsinki also attracts a healthy core of young people. Part of its appeal is the two steambaths below the bar. Open anytime the bar is, the baths show their age and usually are none too clean, but the charge is more than fair: $1.50; $1.75 if the bar supplies towel and soap.

I heartily recommend the Helsinki in any tour of Butte. Drinks are cheap (draft beer — thirty cents). The ambience is as ethnic as you're likely to get. You can dance, drink, sing or cry in your beer. No one will bother you. And if you're just a little lucky, an old man may walk through the door blowing a bugle.

Charley's New Deal Bar

333 South Arizona
Butte

At eleven in the morning the long bar at Charley's New Deal is more populated than it often is in early evening. Pictures crowd the walls — pictures of football and baseball teams so old the uniforms seem as strange as men's two-piece bathing suits. Pictures of Halloween parties Charley has thrown for the children of Butte for close to 30 years, pictures of various Democratic presidents. Pictures thick on the old, yellow-green walls, like memorabilia from 100 grandmothers' living rooms. A silver bust of a noble FDR looks over the melee from above the bar.

At one end of the old wood plank a union man, just off shift, is cracking peanuts and sipping a draft while reading the *Montana Standard.* A young lawyer, a friend of Charley's son, Mike, is drinking coffee. At the other end of the bar, middle-aged and elderly drunks congregate. Marinated for years in drafts and straight shots, they don't know morning from night.

Esther, Charley's petite, solemnly gracious wife, is tending bar. When she leaves for lunch her youngest son, 22-year-old Mark, takes over, exhibiting the family aptitude for bartending that has kept some regulars coming in more than 30 years. And Charley himself shuffles in, a heavy, gregarious figure, gnarled and wise from all those years behind the plank.

Charley spent a good part of his childhood in Butte, but he was on his way to Nevada in 1936 when he stopped in Butte to give his friend, Esther, a hand with her father's bar. He was going to Nevada to get in on the "gambling business." At that time Butte was the gambling spot in the West. Las Vegas was soon to siphon off Butte's Meaderville trade, but Butte was still the Big Time in the '30s. It had every sin a man or woman might hope to indulge in. And it had jobs for everyone.

Then the New Deal was not an ancient red brick building, its fancy front peeling, deserted by other buildings its age. South Arizona was once as busy a street as any in Butte. Now the New Deal stands abrupt and strangely alone against the skyline, a parking lot on one side, the street winding down to 1940ish buildings.

Two and three-storied 19th century brick, like most of old Butte, used to stand on both sides of Charley's. Charley said there was a Scandinavian bar called the Half Way House nearby, and a shop with women barbers, and what was called a slave market (now progressively labeled the Job Service). Across from Charley's was the Cabbage Patch, that infamous section of Butte where people down on their luck or plagued by one addiction or another, lived in tents and shacks and facetiously chose their own King and Queen. Now seedy grey apartment complexes built to house copper workers during World War II sit across from Charley's.

But the New Deal lives on and unlike many other Butte landmarks, its demise does not seem imminent. With Charley's son Mike holding down the heavy night shift, continuity and tradition seem assured.

Charley and Esther Judd have four sons. The family reflects Charley and Esther, as well as Butte. The eldest, much to Charley and Esther's pride, recently was ordained a Catholic priest. Mike tends bar at the New Deal. Martie is a beer distributor in Utah, and the youngest, Mark, deals cards in Las Vegas when he's not helping with the New Deal.

But then the New Deal always has been a family bar. Esther's father ran a bootlegging business out of the building during Prohibition. A grocery store front provided the cover, but bootlegged whiskey was the real source of revenue. With the lifting of Prohibition it was back to the bar again, named for FDR's social innovations. The name still fits the Democratic, working-man's town.

Charley tells me, "There have only been three men in the world — Jesus, Roosevelt and myself." Charley's father also was a bartender, he tells me, when he wasn't out prospecting, or dealing cards, or "running all over the West chasing the buck." Charley's dad ran the famous Mint Cafe in Great Falls for a time.

The Mint Cafe, so the stories go, is where Charlie Russell hung out, drawing with his now-acclaimed style the scenes of Indians and cowboys on napkins or any other available surface and turning them over to just about anyone for a free drink. Charley touches on another common story told about Russell — "He never amounted to anything until he got married. She took him out of the bars, put him in a log cabin, and told him to draw."

Ah, Charley can tell you lots of things: stories about Butte; about the toughest Butte bar ever, the Bowery, on the corner of Granite and Colbert; about the Bar of Justice, run by a "notorious bunch of sons a guns" who ended up in the pen in Deer Lodge; how Friggy McQuinn stole enough votes to elect Jim Murray; how when Charley was a young lad — 9 or 10 — boys would walk up the hill to where, for five cents, a colored lady would lift up her skirt and dance — "for another five cents she'd do other things."

While I'm talking to Charley, no less than three drunks

approach him for free liquor. One poor man wants to buy a pint with forty cents. Charley, obviously a soft touch, holds up against the barrage until the man finally saunters weak-kneed out the door. Another man, quite young, approaches Charley respectfully, acting like he's going for a loan at the bank. "Esther always lets me have a pint at the end of the month," he begins. "The end of the month — this is the 10th," Charley points out. The man says he needs it a little early this month; that Esther *usually* gives it to him.

Charley questions that and by this time the man is even more respectful. It's like he's talking to a priest. He asks again for the pint, and Charley, chuckling, says, "Can Jesse James get an installment at the Time Pay?" Finally Charley tells Mark to give the man a half pint. Charley tells the third intruder, "Not now, I'm right in the middle of a business deal — about to sign the papers."

Every Halloween since 1942 Charley has thrown a Halloween party for the kids of Butte. Halloween 1978 I stop by. The bar is closed; no liquor is served. The place is bursting with kids of all sizes. Tables are stretched the length of the long room. Costumed children, most of them escorted by their parents or grandparents, walk through the line as adults scoop candy, apples and popcorn into their sacks.

Halloween in the New Deal

A smile rarely leaves Charley or Esther's face. In fact, everyone smiles. The place is full of smiles. Mike walks up to me. He points to two middle-aged women at the front of the candy line. He says the same women have had that same position since before he can remember. He says there used to be many neighborhoods with lots of children around the New Deal, but those were in busier days, before the pit began to eat into the uptown. Now the parents have to drive their kids to the New Deal. But still they come.

The Judds get close to 1,000 kids through their doors Halloween night. And usually someone is taking pictures, as the walls of Charley's testify. Large blown-up black and whites crowd each other for room.

"Where's last year's party?" I asked Mike one night. "We've got it," he said. "We just don't have room to put it up." One year Charley had close to 3,000 parents and kids. And one year he was so overcome with the revelry of the occasion he went outside to set off some firecrackers; they went off too soon and he landed in the hospital with 10 stitches in his head.

Following the '79 kids' party, the New Deal hosted the older kids of Butte, the 25 to 35 age bracket, in a wild, costumed revelry that had been announced only by word of mouth. The music was jazz/rock piano and drum. The dancing could best be described as spontaneous. Charley sat in a corner surveying the scene, his usual broad grin reduced to a ghost of a smile. Perhaps he was seeing the 30-year-olds coming through the candy line 20 years before.

o—O—o

Charley operates a take-out liquor store, boasting a fine selection of wines. And he sells milk, eggs and bread, too. Mike says they do a remarkable business with milk. He says the guys don't like to walk into the house empty-handed after being out late. If they're carrying a carton of milk when they come in the door, they at least can say, "Well, I just stopped by the New Deal to pick up some milk, and . . . ."

The New Deal is the kind of bar that takes on different personalities through the day. In the morning and early afternoon the old regulars are there, and friends of the family come to chat with whomever is behind the bar. At noon teenagers from Butte High descend on the bar, ordering cokes and potato chips. Night shift men drink at the New Deal through the day, but since Mike returned from Missoula to bartend, late night attracts a young crowd.

I'm a New Deal regular. I go there once or twice a week.

Whenever I'm there — if only to buy a bottle of wine for dinner — a couple of drinks are bought for me. If Mike doesn't buy the second, he buys the third. Usually a few friends are in, and there're a couple more drinks.

Midnight at the New Deal on almost any night will find a strange combination of old regulars and a crowd of what might be called Butte's younger generation of Bohemians, a sort of community in itself in a town that is growing old and can do little to attract young people. Late nights at the New Deal sometimes remind me of the late Eddy's Club in Missoula, where in the 1960s and early '70s, a crowd of journalists, artists, would-be philosophers, college students and hopeless degenerates shared tables in the blare of flourescent lights under a remarkable photographic collection. The conversation and flow of ideas rarely seemed to slow.

Eddy's often was very dirty; quite raucous; foreign to people who didn't understand it. But it was a rarity — a bar for a bar's sake — where you almost always found an old friend or made a new one. A bar to talk in, spit on the floor in, read a magazine in, do as you pleased in. Without pretense or camouflage. If you liked Eddy's you felt as good there at two in the afternoon as at closing time.

The New Deal is like that. And more. It's a Butte bar. It reflects the dual character of the town: a harshness bordering on cruelty sometimes found in its people, so much of their town and their past lost to the ever-growing grey-ugly pit; that fatalism bred of a company town; the extremity of the weather; the frustrating disappointment of years of economic decline; easily overcoming all of that, the generosity, loyalty and warmth of a people who have learned that friends and neighbors are more valuable than all the ore taken from what, after 100 years of mining, is still called the richest hill on earth.

The Met Tavern
1375 Harrison Avenue
Butte

If the M&M is grandfather of Butte bars, the Met sired the next generation. The Met is a sport bar, a working man's bar, a card players' bar, a singles' bar and a good place to eat lunch.

Owner Bobby Pavlovich serves sandwiches, soup and specials during the week. Tuesday is a popular day; prime rib is served at noon. It's best to get there a little before noon, to be sure they don't run out before they get to you.

Some days customers cook for the bar. The day I'm in visiting with Bobby, he tells me a regular is planning on making minestrone soup for the house the next week. "Somebody wants to cook, they cook," affable Bobby says. "They make enough for everybody and we pay 'em."

Like the M&M, the Met has a large clientele that spans age and interest barriers. But it probably is best known as a sport bar. A ticker tape in the card room provides up to the minute sports scores from across the country, and the bar's sports pools always are a favorite topic of conversation.

Bobby can't think of anything too special about his bar, except the Olympic Brewery formerly stood where the Met now stands. The brewery was moved to Seattle and the Met was built in 1948.

Bobby remembers the night Evel Knievel barhopped through Butte. According to stories of two bartenders who worked that night, Evel had talked of hosting a party for Butte to celebrate before the Idaho Falls jump. Typically compulsive, Evel decided tonight was *the* night. He called Muzz and Stan's Freeway Bar to say he was on his way. The party began there and was carried to the Acoma, the Met, and finally, the El Mar. Evel bought drinks all the way. The crowd went with him from place to place, often spilling onto the sidewalks outside the bars. Bobby says the Met was "jammed to the eyeballs." He estimates Evel spent about $1,500 in each bar — a cool six grand. Evel's idea of a Butte six-pack.

The Deluxe on East Front is a choice Butte joint, with a door that looks like a barricade and the reasons for that are clearly stated inside. I would venture to say the Deluxe has the best sandwiches for the price in the country — ham, turkey, beef — sliced thin, piled at least an inch high — as well as spicy kolbasa, on a choice of three breads, with lettuce if you like — for $1.25.

The **Five Mile** on Harrison Avenue is a classic roadhouse bar, built long before Butte began to stretch out onto the flat. Packy Buckley's **Club** on West Broadway is a favorite of many, especially on St. Patrick's Day and during the Christmas season, when Packy serves the best Tom and Jerry's in town.

Muzz & Stan's Freeway on South Montana serves tasty fried chicken and fish and chips and sometimes hosts old miners who sing to the bar old underground mining songs . . . "Oh, my sweetheart's a mule in the mine . . ."

You might want to stop in the **El Mar** on Harrison Avenue, Butte's cowboy stomping grounds, often a good place to dance. The El Mar is rather erratic in booking bands. Some are exceptional (for Montana, anyway); others would offend a howling coyote. And then some you just find hard to believe. For weeks the El Mar boasted a group with a sort of Las Vegas big band sound; featured was a midget trumpet player who wore either a pale pink tutu or a baby blue tutu.

If you're feeling particularly adventuresome, stop in Dirty-Mouth Jean's **Stockman Bar** on Galena street uptown. Probably the most notorious of Butte bars, the Stockman was run for years by Dirty Mouth Jean, who killed a young G.I. on his way home from bootcamp. A fight had ensued when she refused to serve the guy's black friend. She was convicted in 1979.

The Owl
819 East Third
Anaconda

Old photos of Montana saloons show men bellied up to the bar, foot on the rail, no bar stool in sight. A bar stool in the old saloons was as likely as the proverbial teats on a mule. I'm not sure when the stool was introduced, but I have a theory.

With Prohibition, many of the bars took to selling ice cream, Hire's rootbeer and other such frivolous refreshments. The old photos confirm Montana pioneers believed alcohol was made for drinking standing up, but it must have seemed silly to stand, foot on the rail, to sip a soda or dig into a mound of ice cream. The bar stool came in with ice cream and soda pop, I will contend, and the furniture remained after Prohibition ended. Today it is difficult to find a saloon without the stools.

But the past dies slowly in Anaconda. There I found a bar where stools have neither seen the light of flourescent bulbs, nor felt the spray of a draft: The Owl on Third Street.

Butte copper magnate Marcus Daly built Anaconda practically overnight, the town he needed to house the workers for his copper smelter. He also built an electric streetcar system to carry the workers to and from work. The streetcars ran down Third Street, stopping every two blocks. At every one of these stops at least one bar flourished; many survive to this day — the Owl, the Mill, Sladich's.

The proprietors of Sladich's and the Owl vie for the distinction of oldest Anaconda bar. Dick Barkell of the Owl says he has a title dated 1893 for the Owl's building. Mautz

Sladich shows me clippings from his family's grand opening in 1896, cautioning "other" bars in Anaconda might not have the proof to back up their claims.

Beyond this version of sibling rivalry, both bars are worth a visit. Standing foot on the rail at the Owl — a rail that has supported men dead 80 years — is an experience akin to standing on a cliff once used as a buffalo jump or following the Missouri along the route of Lewis and Clark.

Across from the bar are old oak tables and chairs where old men who no longer can stand for any length of time sit proud and upright, vague smiles on their faces. Behind them is an old oak shuffleboard that hasn't been used for years, but will not be moved for many more years. The reason for its not being moved has more to do with indifference than with a desire to exhibit one of the bar's antiques. (Customers tell me the shuffleboard came up on the steamboat to Fort Benton, like so many of Montana's old back bars. That would make it more than 100 years old.)

The Owl might be the oldest bar operating in the same location still in business in Montana. It probably has changed less than any of the bars competing for the distinction. And it's done it without making any point of it. The Owl doesn't bother itself with differentiating the past from the present.

A large side room in the Owl is furnished with straight-back wood booths. Booths probably were built in the side room for the ladies after the 1907 Montana Legislature passed a bill outlawing women "entertaining" in saloons. The booths are equipped with buzzers used to summon the barkeep.

The buzzers and the booths are intact the afternoon I stop in, but all the action is in the main room. The Owl's back bar is old, nondescript. The brass beer drain looks new, although it's probably about as old as the bar. The plank is wood, worn smooth. The rail is beaten grey metal. Spittoons are positioned next to it about every four feet. They're used more as ashtrays now than for chew. Even then, patrons have missed more often than they have hit the mark. There's plenty of snacks for purchase. It's the first time I've seen Sen-Sen on sale for a while.

Bartender Dick is friendly, accommodating. The guys standing around me say he runs a "clean joint." I ask Dick about an organization formerly associated with the Owl, the Breakfast Club. Dick laughs and tells me he belonged. Weshy Beausoliel (pronounced Bushly in Anaconda) managed the Owl in the 1950s. His son, Joe, told me how the Breakfast Club started.

Weshy was a devout Catholic who liked to get his friends

together for a chat on Sunday morning. At that time bars weren't allowed to open on Sunday until two in the afternoon. Every Sunday after 8 a.m. Mass, Weshy would open the Owl to his friends, those friends who had attended Mass.

Weshy usually knew the men who could be depended on to make Mass, so he wouldn't question them. Those he wasn't sure about would be greeted at the door. Weshy would quiz them: "Who said Mass? What was the sermon? The gospel?"

If they passed the test they joined the club for its early morning meeting. The men sat in the side room in the booths. Bartenders were Joe, who was in gradeschool at the time, and his two brothers.

Joe spent a good part of his childhood around the Owl. He remembers there was always talk of cleaning the place up, redecorating. The decision always was made against it because the men off work from the smelter carried with them the residue of their work and the last place they wanted to drink in was a place that made them feel even dirtier than they were.

Joe also remembers when beer prices increased: "The men really got bent out of shape when beer went from a nickel to a dime (some time in the 1950s)." Today an Owl draft is thirty-five cents. In the old days, a few minutes before the shift change at the smelter, the bartender would begin lining up shots of whiskey and beer chasers (called Sean O'Farrells in Butte-Anaconda) to be ready for the men who poured en masse from the streetcar doors.

When the shift changes at four, many of today's smeltermen board a bus that replaced the streetcars. The bus makes the same stops the streetcar established before the turn of the century. When the men walk in the door of the Owl, a bottle and a beer chaser are there to greet them. Dick puts the bottle on the bar and the men pour their own shots. Three shots and a beer chaser go for $1.55. This low price is in line with prices in many of the old bars in Butte-Anaconda where any bar worth its salt buys every third drink.

Nowhere else in the state is that after-work drink revered as it is in Butte-Anaconda. There is a deep-seated trust in both towns that whiskey, after a shift of breathing rock dust underground, or fighting the fumes of the smelter, is as medicinal as a weekly dose of camphor oil. That first well-earned shot purges the throat, brings a cleansing tear to the eye, fights its way down through the weary, embattled throat and lungs, right down to the abdomen where it settles in a warm, healing pool, and from there sends out a message to the brain that all is much righter with the world than it was an hour before. Another shift has been pulled.

I'm having a nice conversation with some elderly men, most of them retired from smelter work. Anaconda is one of a few towns in the country where, when you ask the number of employees at a given place, the person responds with a question: "day's pay or salary?" I have to make sure I know the difference first, and then I'm told, about 700 day's pay, about 300 salary. (A poor copper market and other factors have led to extensive lay-offs in Anaconda as well as in Butte over the last few years. At one time there were 15,000 miners in Butte alone. Now less than 2,000 are employed in the open copper pit; the underground mines were closed in 1974.)

Dick drops by occasionally to throw out more interesting tidbits about the Owl. It was first run by Black Mike, who was nicknamed Black Mike not because he was dastardly, but because he was dark-haired and dark complected. Black Mike had a chute built into the side of the bar, where barrels of beer were delivered. Dick claims the Owl is the only bar in the state that still handles the full 32-gallon barrels of beer. Everyone else gets the 16-gallon kegs. Dick gets the barrels because he goes through so much beer in a week — about 18 barrels, or 576 gallons. Nine barrels are delivered twice a week. The barrels are less trouble because only one of the nine has to be tapped.

Above the Owl's cash register is the shrine-like photograph of Franklin Roosevelt found in almost every old bar in Butte-Anaconda. I've always connected the ever-present representation of FDR in Butte with FDR's success in lifting the country from the Great Depression. In Sladich's I'm given another perspective.

Sladich's

600 East Third
Anaconda

The first thing I see in Mautz Sladich's place is a full color portrait of FDR sitting over the cash register. I tell Mautz that it seems I find FDR in every bar in Butte and Anaconda. "Sure," says Mautz, "that's because he gave the country back to booze." Three men drinking at the bar form a chorus in agreement, rather surprised I could be so dense.

Although Sladich's has been renovated and little of the old is left in the decor, the family has owned the building and the bar since before the turn of the century. Mautz has old time photos and paraphenalia to prove it. Most of it is in what he calls the garbage case.

Some of the antiques and collectibles in the case were brought in by Sladich's patrons, but much of it was gathered by the family. There's a "Keep Cool with Coolidge" sign in the case; photos of the bar's grand opening in 1896; an old harmonica; an English leather cribbage board; a button hook, a raffle ticket from 1897 (Mautz's grandfather paid a dollar for the ticket; an $85 bicycle was raffled.)

There's an 18-inch Nazi dagger in a scabbard and a Nazi Cross, both of which Mautz claims he took off dead Nazis, along with some authentic Hitler stamps. Have Mautz give you a little tour through the case; he enjoys it.

Toward the end of my tour I notice a full-size American flag folded in the classic style in the case. I ask Mautz about it. It was the flag draped over the casket of a close friend. The man was a bachelor who spent a good deal of time with Mautz in the bar. Sladich's was probably as close to home as any place for the man, and Mautz was his best friend. When the man died Mautz took care of the funeral arrangements and, since there was no widow to claim it, Mautz was given the flag.

Sladich's isn't nearly as crowded as the Owl, perhaps because it is so clean; more likely, it's because Mautz closes at six. It's his bar and he's not getting any younger. He feels like closing at six, so he closes at six. But while he's open, it would be difficult to find a bartender more gracious than this laughing Croatian. With nearly every shot he pours for one of his friends, Mautz pours one for himself. I begin to feel the only reason Mautz is open at all is to meet with his friends. During the hour I spend with him, I see him tip many shots; yet any effect the liquor could be having on him is not apparent. He is one of the healthiest-looking 60-year-old men I've seen.

With every shot comes a toast. His customers may forget, but Mautz never does. Ritual, grace, style, brotherhood: with every tip of the glass, Mautz salutes life. The toasts varied that day, but the most common was, "Happy Days."

Helena-Deer Lodge

Corner Bar

402 Main Street
Deer Lodge

I'm talking to one of the last sheepherders in Montana —
Fred Lenning — a nearly toothless, good-natured old guy who
frequents the Corner Bar in Deer Lodge when he's not out
watching sheep.

Fred remembers one day when Deer Lodge was celebrating
its annual rodeo. Fred was a young boy, standing outside the
Corner Bar. His father was a gambling man, tending business
inside the bar. A cowboy rode up to young Fred and bet him
$10 he couldn't ride his horse through the bar. Fred took the
guy up on the bet, jumped on the horse, and was making good
headway through the bar when his father spotted him.

Fred's dad strode up to the horse, yelling at his son all the
way; when he reached them he grabbed the horse's tail and

yanked on it in an attempt to stop the two and discipline Fred. When he learned his son was in the process of winning $10, the man dropped the horse's tail and congratulated his boy.

Fred retired a number of years ago. He's worked at various jobs, including a long stint as a garbageman. Before his father gambled it away, the family had owned a large sheep ranch, so it was logical for one of the last sheep ranchers in the valley to ask Fred if he was available to watch sheep.

Fred's boss is the last real sheep rancher in the Deer Lodge Valley, according to Fred — the only man who runs as much as a band of sheep (about 1,000 head). A young man would have trouble living on the $400 Fred earns a month, but with his pension, he says he does fine. "The pension is good if you don't come in here," Fred tells me.

What's it like to watch sheep for days on end?

It's great work for a man his age, Fred says. For several months of the last five or six years, he has lived in a sheep wagon, following the sheep as they move to greener pastures. He has trouble with coyotes and shoots one whenever he gets the chance, but agrees with those who think the controversial poison 1080 should be banned. Fred thinks sheep ranchers should have sheepherders watching their flocks unless they want to take the losses.

What does he do the weeks he's with the sheep? "I watch sheep, sit on a rock, eat, watch sheep, read a paper if he (his boss) brings it, sit on a rock, watch sheep . . . ."

The Corner is a rough, ugly old-timer's bar. Like most of the bars that have survived for nearly a century — like Fred Lenning for that matter — the Corner can't manage a prettiness; it's too old. But it can tell some stories. A few are told on the walls. One high quality blown-up photo framed and hung on the wall opposite the bar intrigues me. Five bobcats are strung up — hung like outlaws — over the wood plank sidewalk of a bar in Helmville. The photo was taken in 1952. At that time bobcats were overrunning the valley, killing cattle and sheep, according to a couple of old-timers in the bar. There was a bounty on them, so the men who killed these five were proud of their take.

The Corner's back bar is unique in my travels. A square stained-glass motif in green and yellow is inlaid through the long, oak casing of the back bar and accompanying lights. The back bar and matching plank and liquor cabinets are solid oak, made by Brunswick around the turn of the century, first used in the Crystal Bar in Anaconda.

The plank is systematically scarred, etched throughout with deep nicks. I'm told by the bar owner, Henry Meagher, that the nicks came from customers pounding their coins into the wood in an attempt to get the barkeep's attention. Henry Meagher is a descendant of Montana's first territorial governor, Thomas Meagher, the charismatic Irishman who reportedly fell off the dock and drowned at Fort Benton one night while in an intoxicated state. Henry claims to know little, if anything, about the man, although he does say he is related to him in some way.

I've had a fine afternoon with the old-timers in the Corner, but it's time to push on. Fred Lenning says he's about ready to go, too. He's due to begin several weeks with the woolies. He tells me a young guy has been watching them, but the guy can't stay out too long. He likes to be in town for the weekends to chase the girls. Fred doesn't mind missing weekends in town, he says, adding he's too old to chase the women. Then with a sly grin, he puts in a word for the sheep: "I like them four-legged blondes."

Ting's
Jefferson City

In the late 19th century, goods and people were moved in the West by stagecoach. About every 12 miles the teams had to be changed. So every 12 miles in the run between Helena, Virginia City and Butte, there was a stage stop. Nearly all these stage stops were equipped with bars.

Jefferson City and what is now called Ting's bar was the first stop out of Helena. The second team carried the coach to

Boulder, then down the valley to Virginia City, over to Butte and back. Just about every 12 miles between Helena and Butte a traveler today finds either a small town or a bar where the stage once stopped — Jefferson City, Boulder, Basin, Elk Park.

I'm in Ting's, talking to Whale (pronounced Wally) Phelan, grandson of one of the settlers of the Boulder Valley. He remembers hearing about the stage run and how his grandfather broke a new horse to pull for it nearly every day. There was a real demand for strong, dependable horses then. He said a 12-horse team was used to freight eastern beer and other goods brought up to Fort Benton by steamboat.

Ting, described by patrons as a "character" and a "politician," died several years ago. There's been some interest in keeping his bar authentic. The walls are the bright red popular around the turn of the century, with a waist-high wood wainscoting. There are mining tools hung around, a few antiques. Sandwiches, chicken and other basics are prepared at the end of the long old mirrored back bar. The poker and keno games are intense.

Travelers between Helena and Butte are a constant clientele. When you think of it, Ting's serves close to the same function today as when those teams of sweating horses pulled up short at the stage stop's door.

The Rialto
52 N. Main
Helena

The well-planned art deco bar of the Rialto, along with a counter cafe and a rambunctious card room in the back, form a fine all-purpose gathering spot in the spirit of the old-time saloon. In Helena, the Rialto comes closest to the community status the M&M Cigar Store enjoys in Butte.

Butte's M&M is large, free-wheeling, often decadent. Anything can happen in the M&M; virtually no one will be surprised. The Rialto is tight, stylistic and orderly, with a wholesome 1950ish air; its clients are easier to surprise.

Like many of the old-time bars, the Rialto began as a cigar store — Goodman's Cigar Store. A fire destroyed a good part of the building in 1928. The structure was rebuilt and used as a barber shop for a short time. Mike Tuohy and two partners bought the building in 1930 and put in the lunch counter, custom-made by Weber Showcase Co. of Los Angeles. When Prohibition ended, they put in the bar. Cigars were sold in front. A large selection was available, all stored in beautiful, wood refrigerated cigar cases.

Tuohy displayed the cases in the window of the cafe for years after they were used. Sadly, the cases were removed when the Rialto changed hands in 1977.

The rounded forms and enclosed light are 1930s art deco. The room is packaged neatly with a three-tier wood trim edging dropped about a foot from the ceiling, something like a ribbon around the room. Tuohy had the back bar custom-made in Helena in Foley's mill. It features back-lighted panels, which give the room a mellow red glow. Half-moon booths line one wall in the miniature bar room, with a large keno cage holding stage on the side.

Keno is big in the Rialto. Cards and gaming always have been big here. The back card room is as large as the cafe and bar together. Heavy gilded frames hold old paintings above the heads of old men at the poker table. They are as much fixtures of the place as the wood trim. Panguigue is the game in the Rialto today; it has been since gambling was outlawed in 1957.

The Rialto is popular among all sorts of Helena people — state workers, construction men, students, drifters, the elderly. Lunch attracts a sampling of the city's citizens. The overflow from the cafe counter is found in the bar and the card room.

The Rialto's food is good, basic fare at a reasonable price. The comfortable class of the place is refreshing after a tour through the noveau chic establishments proliferating in a growing Helena. The Rialto is the kind of place where you can order a beer and a burger at the bar, and not worry about mentioning the slice of raw you want for your burger. It comes without asking.

It's also the kind of place (a friend told me) where you can punch any number of top 20 songs on the jukebox, and hear — regardless of what you punch — a song straight out of the '50s.

Frontier Town
Highway 12 West
Helena

"Only God can make a tree, but I can whittle the hell out of 'em," John Quigley tells me in what may be the best explanation for Frontier Town — a virtual forest of trees he has whittled the hell out of. John built this replica of an early western town nearly single-handedly on a perch of rocky ground near the top of McDonald Pass, taking most of a lifetime to make sure he got it right.

Besides the large lodge and museum, there's a bank, jail, Ma Jones' Corset Shop, a general mercantile, a lovely chapel, and other assorted buildings. The village is built of smooth yellow wood taken from the forest nearby, worked into whatever practical purpose the mind of John Quigley found for it, and varnished to a warm glow.

The buildings are only the beginning. Quigley's passion for wood and ability with natural materials extends to details, such as pine carved picture frames, a finely crafted standing cribbage board and accompanying stools, wood sculpture.

When he doesn't use wood, he uses rock — massive stones and boulders, also found nearby. They form the many fireplaces found in the bar, the dining area and the lodge. The hallway to the dining room is a mosaic of stone worked into steps and walls, a medieval passage of cold rock that opens into an expansive dining area, built totally of uniform log. The tables and chairs are all handcrafted log, as are the wood chandeliers. John estimated he used 525 tons of boulders and 25 miles of logs in construction.

Frontier Town could be called a life passion; obsession may be closer to the truth. An obvious play is made for tourists, but the place transcends tourism, and will outlive Quigley as one man's marvelous obsession. (John Quigley died at the age of 64 of cancer in late 1979. I wrote this after visiting him at Frontier Town in March of the same year.)

But what we are talking about here is bars. Frontier Town has a dandy. By 1953 two places had been used as bars. That year John expanded the lodge and built the present bar. He used a Douglas fir 50 feet long, about four feet in diameter. He found the tree in the woods near Frontier Town, cut it, and then split it clean down the middle. The bottom half became the bar plank; the top, the main ceiling support for the room. Standing back from the bar, one gets the full effect — a 50-foot tree sliced down the middle — one half holding up customers, the other holding up the room.

Hanging on one of the bar's log pillars is the framed photo of Quigley with a bear he killed in 1962. The hapless bear — confused, hungry or perhaps just dumb — had entered the building through the kitchen and found its way down to the bar around closing time one summer night. With his usual dramatic flair, John hung the photo above the spot where the bear died and mounted the bear nearby. Incidents such as that, along with John's habit of wearing a holster and gun, have made him a legend in the area.

A mounted buffalo is stuck away in one dark corner of the bar. John's uncle had a herd of buffalo when John was a boy.

He wanted to get rid of some, so John shot this one and had it mounted. In another corner is a wood sculpture of an Indian brave, his head bent as if listening to the wind. John carved it out of a 9-foot spruce, 38 inches in diameter. The sculpture weighs about 400 pounds.

Hand-crafted wood tables and chairs are spread throughout the room. In an effort to keep his work as authentic as possible John carved his own wood pegs and wedged them into the wood, in lieu of nails. Part of the bar is open, without stools. Another part has eight matching saddles mounted as bar stools.

The room housing the bar is full of interesting antiques and oddities. One cabinet holds gold pans and weights used by Quigley's grandfather, a pioneer Montana merchant. Spread throughout the place are quality antiques, some items the likes of which would be difficult to find in the state's historic museum. A good part of the antiques have been brought in by customers. John has bought only a few, such as the gun that he "bought from an old lady who needed ten bucks."

Many of the articles are relics of Blackfoot City, a long-dead gold mining town that once boasted some 5,000 people, a few miles from present day Avon. John's grandfather, another John Quigley in a generational line of men of the same name that goes back to Ireland, settled in Blackfoot City in the 1880s.

Eventually he was the proprietor of the town's livery stable, a slaughter house, a store and a bar. John has one of his grandfather's ledgers. He says the loans varied from a sack of beans to cash and always listed the nationality of the debtor — white, colored, Chinese, or Indian. Most of the debts were not repaid. Blackfoot gold did not pan out, and the town, like so many other mining settlements, was dead before the doctor diagnosed the illness.

John's father became heir to a good part of the town when his father died. Eventually, he tore down buildings for firewood, but the next John Quigley in line inherited something of his grandfather's spirit.

While his father was tearing down buildings, John was gathering as many of the old tools and household furnishings as he could. And as he watched the final deterioration of his grandfather's town, John Quigley decided he would build another town, a showpiece of pioneer Montana, a town crafted from native material by his own hands, a town to hold the relics of a past receding as quickly as the weeds grew in Blackfoot City's main street.

John's father was a rancher, and he was heir to the family ranch. But his first wife got his part of the ranch when they were divorced. In 1946 John bought what appeared to be a worthless piece of ground on rocky McDonald Pass. He pitched a tent there and began to put his dream to practice, much to the skepticism of the locals. On a trip to Florida John met Sue Whittier. They were married and returned to Montana and a budding Frontier Town. Some 30 years and nine buildings later, John and Sue were still in construction.

In 1975 a fire nearly leveled the dining room. Much of the expansive room has been rebuilt the early spring day I stop in, but John doesn't have a lot of time to talk. He's whittling on his latest project — a reclining bobcat — kept warm by a large wood-burning furnace, built, of course, by John himself.

Downstairs Peter Quigley, John's second son, is tending bar. Most of his customers are cross-country skiers, warming themselves after touring a four-mile trail into the Helena National Forest. The trail starts on Frontier Town's main street.

Hot spiced wine is available, short beers, tasty soups and sandwiches at a reasonable price. Peter is an affable bartender, ready to please, with a folksy, but tough demeanor. He wears a cowboy hat, as does the cook, Helmut, a German emigrant who seems to have taken to the West and Frontier Town like a moth to wool.

He kids me, saying I won't go to town with him and get drunk when he's off shift because I don't like his accent.

Upstairs Sue and I watch John whittle. He tells me about the early days, when gold dust was used as exchange, weighed out on scales at the bar. In those days, the dishonest bartender would grow long fingernails, and when weighing out gold, he'd manage to get a good quantity of dust under his nails. He'd walk off shift a good deal richer than when he came on. Another trick was to vasoline his hair, and then cooly rub gold-dust-laden palms through the greasy locks.

We talk a little about the hard and lonely life of Montana pioneers. A visitor feels the toil and sweat and years of work in

John Quigley at Frontier Town Bar

a walk through Frontier Town. Yet there is a grace and easiness in the smooth, shining, functional wood, the fitted stonework, the clean smell of wood burning, the spontaneous hospitality of the Quigleys.

"You made just about everything here, didn't you?" I ask John one more time. "Yeah," he says, "made everything here but money — and I'm working on that."

The Big Hole and The Beaverhead
Moose Bar
6 North Montana
Dillon

Dillon's Moose Bar houses the first authentic wino pit I've found in my search. The Moose is the epitome of the rough, tough, good time bar. Its wino pit, a sad, small dark room is off to the side in the back. The late afternoon I was there an old man was taking a nap on the floor. Later the room would take on its nighttime personality.

The winos are quite the musicians, the thick, earthy middle-aged woman behind the bar tells me and my friend, Gail. "They buy a bottle or a few cases together and sit in there and do their visitin'. They play their guitars, fiddles. They're educated men who just got lost along the way, with losin' their families and stuff," she says. "The majority is sheepherders."

Across from the Moose's attractive art deco back bar is a mural stretching along a good part of the wall. Drawn in cartoon is a replica of a heavy night at the Moose — drunks rolling dice, a prostitute, a couple of fights, poker.

The Moose has a reputation in Montana for its coarse, devil-may-care ways. A regular tells me, "If you sit here long enough you'll see everything." He said one night a wino pulled out a pistol, stumbled, then dropped the gun. It fired and the bullet caught the bartender in the buttocks.

But this early evening of a hot summer day the Moose is quite relaxed. A dirty-mouthed, obese young woman taunts some older men who sit in theatre seats lined up below the mural. Above the bar are old Schlitz posters in gilded frames and a rendition of "Custer's Last Fight," courtesy of the Anheuser-Busch Brewing Association.

The spittoons built into the foot rest of the bar are used regularly. Draft beer goes for thirty-five cents. Directly in the middle of the shiny wood back bar is a stylistic color overlay on a photo of Steve Logan and his horse, taken in Arizona in 1928. Logan has owned the Moose for years. He wasn't in the day I was, but it's said he always wears black — boots, shirt, pants — with a silver band around his black hat. He used to tend bar with a gun on his hip, which he used when he thought it necessary, which brings us to the story that has made Logan a legend in the area.

One night Logan was trying to close down. A drunk put another dime in the juke box. He didn't live to hear the tune. Montana Liquor Control Board's files note the transfer of the liquor license (in 1969) "to wife's name as he is on trial for shooting a man."

The **Metlen Hotel** sits across the railroad tracks on Dillon's main street. A large, boxlike structure — white trimmed with red — it has a casual class. This summer evening the doors are flung wide open and a soft breeze is cooling the lobby and lounge. The walls are clean, shiny knotty pine. There are dark red furnishings and a healthy growth of plants.

Some 80 years old, the Metlen is a railroader's hotel, but like Dillon and the area — Wisdom, Wise River — there is also a feel of the hunter, sportsman, cowboy and sheepherder about the place. There's more knotty pine in the Dillon area than you'll find anywhere in Montana; and the Metlen's pine is primo.

Hand-carved pine trim frames the oak back bar in the small, low-ceiling lounge. The oak cabinets below the bar are beautiful, built for immortality. Like the Moose, the Metlen has spittoons built into the bar's footrest.

There's a sign tacked to the bar that reads, "Dance at the

Metlen — Live Music Aug. 5." A hand-tooled woman's leather purse in the form of a saddle hangs from the bar. I ask the woman if it's for sale. No, she says, just for display. A shotgun is suspended low from the ceiling above the bar. Hanging from it is a sign saying, "No Bar Credit." We've seen that sign in every bar in Dillon. A few other signs in the Metlen seem to capture the Dillon attitude — "No Shirt, No Shoes, No Booze, No Service;" "Cows May Come and Cows May Go, But the Bull Goes on Forever," and "Halitosis is Better than No Breath at All."

Dillon claims its rodeo over Labor Day weekend makes for the biggest weekend in Montana. If not on the money, they're close. A good part of southwestern Montana can be seen on the cowtown's late-night Labor Day streets. At first glimpse it seems more people are on the streets than could be in the bars. A push through the bars changes the story.

The Moose holds the hard cores and a few natives. The cowboys are in motel rooms getting some sleep so they don't get kicked in the head when they ride the next day. The winos have scattered. The night is left to the amateurs.

We push through the crowd and into the **Crystal.** An old woman is pounding an out-of-tune piano and a crowd gathered around her is singing songs like "A Bicycle Built for Two," "The Sidewalks of New York," and "Don't Fence Me In." The small, straightshot of a bar rocks with the piano player's foot on the peddle and the boots that thump the floor to the simple, solid rhythm.

One of the singers — about 250 pounds of rich rancher — spots a friend coming in the door. Realizing his friend won't be able to see him, the big guy climbs up on his knees on a small, circular table next to the piano. The crowd is wary. The man balances, and somehow stands up on the table. There's a collective sigh of relief. The guy has caught his friend's eye. He tips his hat to him. The friend joins the party, and the singing bursts with more exuberance from the collective windpipe of so many happy people . . . .

Wisdom & Wise River

A few other notable establishments are found in Wisdom and Wise River on Route 43. The Wise River Club and the Wisdom Inn harken back to the days of the gentleman hunter. It's said Butte's Copper Kings, Marcus Daly and William A. Clark, traveled to Wisdom on hunting outings into the Pintler

Mountains. Today there's a healthy traffic of sportsmen and tourists in this area, but they seem to make little impact on the slow, rural pace of either town.

The Wise River Club appeals more to the tourist than the **Wisdom Inn,** a funky old building that new owners have coated with bark in an attempt to enhance its western appeal. Any attempts to impress the tourist are forever suspended inside. The place is more a cluttered, musty taxidermy than a bar. All kinds of stuffed birds, ducks, squirrels, owls, beavers, geese, eagles — thickly coated with dust and age — are propped on tables, shelves and an old upright piano. Old mining and farming tools and guns hang from the ceiling. In the corner of the main room is a tiny closet-like room with bars instead of a door. A sign above the bars says, "JAIL." A woman mannequin is propped up against the wall dressed partly in inmate's clothing. Around her are more dead animals, beaver skins, a single snowshoe.

There's a vintage liberty bell hanging from the ceiling. A sign on a pinball machine promises a free bottle of whiskey for the highest pinball game of the month.

The **Wise River Club,** with its water-hydrant-yellow paint job and buckboard sitting on the roof, is a natural tourist draw. A few wooden Indians are propped up in front. Despite its garish front, the Wise River is a classic old hunter's lodge, with a room in the back stocked with comfortable old couches, chairs, and a wood-burning stove. The bar is made of log planks. Knotty pine throughout the place gives it a fresh, clean feel. A stuffed jackalope is on display to dispel any tourist doubts. Above the bar hang old button shoes, a nice collection of old lanterns, mining hats, antlers. Amidst all the antiques rides a foot-long half-inflated Goodyear blimp.

The Longbranch and
The Silver Dollar
Ennis

A few old timers were sitting in the Silver Dollar in Ennis one afternoon. One guy was bragging about his encounters with a certain woman. The woman heard of it, came straight to the bar, pulled out a pistol and shot the guy in the stomach. The man fell out the door of the bar, knelt on the ground holding his stomach, looked at the wound, said, by golly she did shoot me, and fell dead on Ennis' main street. The woman went free.

The Wisdom Inn

The young men relating the incident to me — the Longbranch's friendly bartender and an Ennis local — said the law was on the woman's side, because in Montana "you can't kiss and tell."

The clientele at the Longbranch the hot summer day I was there seemed representative of the people you'll find in the area — a mix of ranchers, easy-going merchants, eastern and Californian fishing enthusiasts, real estate brokers. Outsiders and locals; fishers and cowboys; young and old; all seem to get on just fine in the Longbranch. It's really one of the most jovial bars I've been in. My young friend at the Longbranch tells me they have no trouble with hippies in Ennis. They have long hairs, he says, 'cause it's the style, but real hippies just don't feel at home in Ennis.

The Longbranch and the Silver Dollar are comfortable, clean, unassuming places providing most of the services inherent to a good Montana bar — a full range of alcoholic beverages, pool tables, lots of snacks, food in the back. In the Longbranch rusty, well-worn bridle bits and guns hang above the bar. Elkhorn belt buckles made in Ennis are for sale. Framed pictures of Kitty, Festus and Doc are found on the walls.

They'll cook your trout for you at the Silver Dollar and serve you in a dining room in the back. The afternoon I was there several locals were cooling their throats, shooting pool, dodging the outside's 90 degrees. A middle-aged man asked his woman friend to play the jukebox. She asks what to play. Another woman said, "Just play some from last year — they haven't changed them yet."

Bale of Hay Saloon
336 W. Wallace
Virginia City
(closed winters)

In Virginia City's early days one barkeep would provide a fresh bale of hay for patrons' horses at the hitching post in front of his saloon. The Bale of Hay Saloon it was then; the Bale of Hay today.

Still inhabiting the original building in Montana's oldest living town, the Bale of Hay sits behind a musical arcade, a room crammed with player pianos — player pianos with drums for backup, player pianos with a whole damn band as backup. These instruments, housed in one box, have intricate but sure-fire mechanisms that play not only the piano, but move the bow over the violin strings, and bring the sticks down on the drum: Beautiful reminders from a time when — if you happened to live in Montana and couldn't hear the philharmonic — you got the next best thing.

A small low door opens into one of the most original saloons one is likely to find anywhere. I'm told the back bar is the oldest in Montana — built in Cincinnati in 1862 and shipped up by riverboat.

It seems almost miniature in comparison to the early 20th century grandeur of newer models. Its shining mahogany is intricately carved into knobby spokes and prim circles, and worked with three-inch square mirrors into a pleasing design. The mirrors are peeling, but the wood seems to have been carved yesterday.

Ford Bovey, son of the late Charles Bovey, tells me his father bought the back bar in the 1940s for $50. Charles Bovey, rancher, state senator, lover of Montana history, single-handedly restored Virginia City. Later he was to attribute his investment to a good wheat crop in northern Montana in the 1940s. Ford has managed the Bale of Hay the last 15 years — since he was 21 — and since his father died, he's pretty much owned Virginia City.

Small, compact, old, the Bale of Hay was built when the average height of a man was somewhere around five feet. An ancient wood stove commands space in the center of the main room. A fantastic neo-Victorian nude painting — at least 7 feet by 4 feet in elaborate gilded frame — takes up most of one wall. Ford tells me the artist was a man by the name of Pelligrino — "the most famous nude bar picture painter in America."

From the gold, pressed tin ceiling hangs a glittering 1890 chandelier. The gold-plated National cash register was made in 1894. The wallpaper is not the original stuff, but it's old enough to be. Bovey found it still in rolls in another building and had it hung in the Bale of Hay.

Pornographic nickelodians. That's right. Right here in the Bale of Hay. A nickel and a turn of the arm on oak-boxed moving picture devices give a customer a look at lewd scenes, strange situations. Men and women together; women together; all sorts of folks together, and brown-toned frames fluttering by as one turns the handle, leaving the viewer slightly short of breath at the end, surprised at the old folks.

A few steps up from the main room is another drinking nook — low ceiling, no windows, old oak tables, heavy captain's chairs. The place smells old. With a faint tug at the imagination one can smell the yeast from the bread dough. This room once was part of what Ford says is the oldest building in Virginia City. It was a mechanical bakery, mechanical meaning they used a machine to stir the dough.

It was here they shot scenes with Dustin Hoffman for *Little Big Man*. Ford has been involved in several movies filmed in Montana, including *Missouri Breaks*, with Brando and Nicholson. Nicholson loved the Bale of Hay, Ford says, still calls it his favorite saloon.

Tourists don't stay long in the Bale of Hay. They poke their heads in; maybe take a walk through. That's about it. Ford confirmed my suspicions. His clientele is more local than tourist.

The Bale of Hay is a little too real. Its furnishings are rich, elaborate for their time. But they are neither pretty nor comfortable in any modern sense. There's barely room to turn around. You have to sit back in one of the heavy oak chairs to really feel the place; and then the feeling hints of villainy, darkness and death — thieves and murderers — Sheriff Henry Plummer and the gang — and the avenging vigilantes. The air is thick, the rooms musky and dark, lit in high afternoon by one short window.

Bob's Place
Virginia City

Bob Gohn is blind and you wouldn't call his face pretty, but he mixes a good drink and runs his place better than most seeing men manage theirs.

When Bob was a young man — like most men living in Virginia City — he tried his luck in the mines. It was a gold and silver mine, the year 1920. Drilling into the rock, he hit a missed hole, (a hole loaded with dynamite that was "missed" in the original blast). That's how he "got blasted" as he describes it. Surprisingly enough he lived through it, but they had to put his face back together, and his sight was long gone.

Shortly after the accident Bob got into the bar business, running Virginia City's Pioneer for 17 years before taking over Content Corner in 1943, renaming it Bob's Place.

The front of Bob's is a grocery store; the back a bar. Bob sells just about everything — a lot of cigarettes — Bel Air, please — he goes right to the spot. Without the hint of a grope he pulls a package of Bel Airs from a rack holding about 20 brands.

Barbecued potato chips, please. Bob pulls them off a clip

rack. Post cards, baked beans, cinnamon gum. You name it, he's got it; more than that, he can find it in a flash.

It's said that the Internal Revenue Service sent a man to Bob's Place to check on his exemption for blindness. Seeing him operate, the IRS told the regional office Bob was not blind and should be disallowed the exemption. Bob offered to send them his glass eye as proof (the other socket is sewn shut). They left him alone.

My partner Steve and I are ready for a drink. A shot of Jack Daniels, coke back, and a gin and tonic please. Right to the spot, Bob pulls out the gin, takes a shot glass, holds it to his ear, tips the bottle and pours gin to the top of the jigger. He hears it fill. Not a drop is spilled. Now the tonic from the cooler under the bar. Then the bourbon; a coke from the back cooler. He puts the appropriate drinks on the counter in front of us.

A buck sixty-five, he says. Steve and I jump. We dig for our wallets only to realize we have no change.

Steve tells Bob the bill he is handing him is a twenty. Bob's hands move up and down the bill, but to our relief he doesn't hesitate as he rings up the cash register. He's got friends who watch out for him, one of them now visiting with us at the bar. Bob counts out the change from the twenty, and we talk a little.

He says there were seven bars as well as a brewery, operating in Virginia City when he was a kid.

Virginia City had a population of nearly 10,000 in the late 1860s, but gold and silver mining have never made for what could be called a stable community. Now Virginia City seems to be a nicely restored ghost town. But the smattering of locals insist Virginia City never has been a ghost town. People have always lived here, they say; it's the county seat, after all.

They'll tell you that folks have been buying their groceries at Content Corner from Bob Gohn for more than 30 years; before that they bought them from his grandfather, Robert Vickers. Does that sound like a ghost town?

Happily, that feeling permeates the town. The tourists who pound down Virginia City's wooden sidewalks and narrow 19th century streets take the town on the locals' terms.

Bob's other grandfather, George Gohn, was a righteous man — one of Virginia City's pioneers — and a vigilante.

Bob's Place, or Content Corner (named for its second owner, Solomon P. Content) is one of the oldest standing buildings in Montana. John DeHaas described it in his book on historical Montana architecture. For a time — around

1865 — it housed the territorial government's offices. The Governor's office spread across the front of the second floor.

Now the second floor is rented as apartments, and downstairs, Bob Gohn — vigilante's grandson, blinded miner — tends bar and sells supplies.

Paradise and The Park

If I were to choose a town to be stranded in for a weekend, it would be Livingston. The town as 23 bars, many of them classics in their field.

Livingston
The Mint Bar & Liquor Store

102 North Main

The Mint is a railroader's bar. A mural of a ferocious Northern Pacific stretches the length of the long bar. Smaller railroad shots bedeck the walls. Old men seem its main clientele, probably retired railroaders. They harken back to a time when railroading was a promising future for a young man.

The Mint is a tribute to those men; in fact its clientele and its efficient orderliness make it seem a little like the boiler room of a Northern Pacific steam engine.

There's a cafe and cardroom in the back.

The Longbranch Saloon and the Wrangler
117 West Park

The Longbranch Saloon and the Wrangler offer the best in get-down country music and local flavor. Three bars in Livingston — the Wrangler, the Longbranch and Calamity Jane's — have live music two or three nights a week (not bad for a town of about 10,000 population). The bartender at the Longbranch tells me Bozeman college students drive to Livingston on the weekends because they're likely to find more fun on a Livingston Saturday night.

The Longbranch has an interesting collection of Montana brands and photos of the original cast of Gunsmoke as well as some nice blown-up shots of Calamity Jane, the town's favorite daughter.

Calamity Jane's
106 East Park

Calamity Jane's is the prettiest bar I've found on my search. Its back bar is easily the most impressive modern back bar in Montana. Built a few years ago by Craig Zakovi of Bozeman, the bar is done in rich mahogany — a triple arch, rounded and pillored in Romanesque simplicity. Oak captain's chairs complement the back bar. A gaming room behind the bar boasts an upraised poker area, with similar substantial wood furniture.

Owner of the bar and gaming room, Morris Blakeley, tells me he built the poker room because he likes to play himself: "I hated to play in poker rooms that smell bad, so I decided to build one myself." Morris hires women to deal the cards, and he plays poker about every day.

The Sport
114 South Main

Antique buffs will enjoy a visit to the Sport. Besides the 1909 oak back bar, with the original stained glass windows in attending cabinets, there's an ornate player piano with stained glass front, miscellaneous old western tools and equipment — a rusty scythe, a primitive cattle de-horner, cracking leather saddle bags — and a collection of newspapers that scream out the main events of American history in half

page headlines.

There's the leather jacket of Jack Hart, a former Sport regular and RCA cowboy who lived to more than 100 years of age. There's the leggin's of Crow Jackson, who helped to bury Custer's men. The walls are packed with authentic western relics — a thousand of them if the Sport's claims are accurate.

The authenticity of the place can't be questioned. Since Ben Smith founded the Sport in 1909 it has remained in the same building, with the same back bar. The present owner, Ernie Meador, says the back bar was donated by Pabst Blue Ribbon under the agreement that Pabst be the only beer served in the bar. During Prohibition Smith carried on with soft drinks, card games and sporting equipment. The Sport was known then for its milkshakes, and Ernie claims it still serves the best shakes in town.Since Ernie has had the place the Sport had been open mainly for dinner — passable Mexican food. It's rather disturbing to see such a fine old saloon operating only as a restaurant.

The Old Saloon

Livingston opens the door to the glorious Paradise Valley, choice pickin' for saloons. Emigrant's Old Saloon is the first roadside attraction. Its turn-of-the-century false front, with a glistening red trim beckons locals as well as tourists.

The Old Saloon was built in 1902 by Ab Armstrong, Emigrant settler. Gold was discovered in Emigrant Gulch in 1864 and was still a going concern at the turn of the century. Gold scales in the Old Saloon would weigh out a miner's gold and the customer would be given credit on his take until it could be properly assayed in Livingston.

In those days the Old Saloon had two card rooms. One poker game became famous in the area. A news clipping hanging on the Old Saloon's wall tells how a man called Kickin' Horse George kept raising the stakes one night in 1910 until he had pocketed $10,000 in one game. Now, $10,000 is a lot of money today. It was a lot more money in 1910. The Old Saloon likes to remember such individual achievements.

Two unrelated developments caused the closure of the Old Saloon. One was the re-routing of the highway on the other side of the river; the other, of course, was Prohibition. Ab told his son, Elmer, not to worry — they'd put the road back on Emigrant's side of the river sooner or later. Some 40 years later they did. Elmer reopened the bar St. Patrick's Day, 1962.

The Saloon's oak back bar and matching liquor cabinets date back to the bar's beginning. A large mirror back stretches the length of the bar. The matching plank is old enough to have a copper and brass sink. The oak wainscoting lining the room looks untouched. The rotund wood burner sitting in the middle of the room radiates a soothing warmth, the bar's only source of heat. Outside is the original wood-plank sidewalk and hitching post.

Red flock wallpaper, a worn wood plank floor, and assorted antiques contribute to the old saloon flavor. The building itself has stood alone, basically unchanged some 80 years, with the same full-windowed front opening to the Absarokas and formidable Emigrant Peak.

Next door is a restored barn and livery stable now housing a steak house. Dave Beck, who bought the Old Saloon a few years ago, originally planned to move the stable in one piece from its former location in Emigrant. That proved impractical. So he carefully unassembled the old stable and re-assembled it next to the Old Saloon.

The inside of the stable is done in fresh, clean wood, but the stalls are intact, providing separate eating areas. The kitchen was once the tack room.

The Livery's reputation for juicy, reasonably-priced steaks is well-earned, and if an old saloon is to be modernized, Beck's approach is one of the best. The past has been retained, but not at the expense of comfort and cleanliness. And the Old Saloon, happily, is as much a locals' bar as a tourist draw. In fact, it's the kind of place where the two might engage in a "meaningful" conversation.

Chico Hot Springs

Turn left at the Old Saloon and you're on the way to one of Montana's oldest geothermal resorts, Chico Hot Springs. Chico's saloon, with its small dance floor and U-shaped bar, is not remarkable, but there is music nearly every weekend and the bar appears to draw a clientele from a good part of the state. The two outside hot pools and the fine cuisine of Chico's dining room add to the natural attraction of the place.

Right around the corner from Chico, going south on the East River Road, is a unique little hole in the wall called the **Wan-I-Gan.** At one time the Wan-I-Gan may have been the smallest all-purpose bar in the state. When I was there a wide range of groceries and supplies were sold in the tiny front room. Across from the crowded shelves was a bar where we ordered a huge breakfast and a couple of beers, and paid about half what we would have paid anywhere else.

Since, the place has changed hands and groceries and supplies are no longer sold, but food still is served at the small bar, as well as in the back room. Gas is pumped and cabins are rented on the side.

Former owner of the Wan-I-Gan, Doris Whithorn, said the name came from an Indian word, meaning a cook's camp box. Wan-i-gan subsequently came to mean a supply boat that follows along a logging craft; hence the Wan-I-Gan, a stranded supply spot on the banks of the Yellowstone River. I wouldn't miss it on a tour of the Paradise Valley.

The Park

If you head straight south on Highway 89 at Emigrant, you're on your way to Gardiner, the western entrance to Yellowstone National Park. Gardiner has several good saloons.

The **Two Bit Saloon** is a huge, four-room expanse, accommodating two bars, a pool area, a dance floor and a seating area for concerts. Rock walls and shining wood constitute the decor. Open only in season (spring and summer) the Two Bit sponsors country western concerts and is viewed by many as the hottest bar in the area.

The **K-Bar** across the street has one of the most extravagant false fronts in Montana. Inside you'll find a classic Montana watering hole, a good place for swapping lies. The **Blue Goose** is a pleasant locals' haven, open winter and summer.

If you're driving down to Cooke City, you might want to stop in at **Hoosier's** and take a look at the back bar. It was built as a replica of the front of the building. The building's front has been changed slightly since the back bar was built. The bar has been in the family for three generations.

At this point, if it's summertime, you're probably ready to climb over the Cooke City Highway. But if you make the trip in the winter, you will enjoy the animals of the park without having to play the insane leapfrog game with the stalled cars of tourists. At Cooke City you can turn around and head back the way you came. This way, not only will you get double enjoyment of Paradise and the Park, but you can visit any saloon you may have missed on the way up.

Charlie Russell Country

Whiskey has been blamed for lots it didn't
do. It's a bravemaker. All men know
it. If you want to know a man, get him
drunk and he'll tip his hand. If I
like a man when I'm sober, I kin hardly
keep from kissing him when I'm drunk.
This goes both ways. If I don't like
a man when I'm sober, I don't want him
in the same town when I'm drunk.
> — **Charlie Russell**

The Club Cigar

208 Central Avenue

Great Falls

Lena Ford shuffles into the American Legion bar every night between 8:15 and 8:30. The guy who runs the Club Cigar had told me wrong. He said it was between 7:15 and 7:30. The bartender at the American Legion had it right the first time, but when I said I heard it was between 7:15 and 7:30, he hesitated and then said, yeah maybe that's right.

So, here I am, skipping a meeting I'm getting paid to attend, drinking wine with two old guys, waiting for Lena. An hour and a half at the Legion — it's 8:22 — and I'm beginning to wonder if you really can set your watch on Lena as people have told me since I arrived in Great Falls. I ask the bartender if he's sure she'll come. Oh yeah, he says, she never misses. A second later the door opens and in shuffles Lena with two friends. The bartender glances at the clock; then mumbles, "seven minutes late."

Lena Ford ran the Club Cigar, a rough and rowdy Indian and cowboy bar, for 40 years; I'm also told she operated one of the town's main houses of prostitution. It's said she would "bankroll" a hoard of ranch hands who frequented the Club Cigar when they got off the range and into town. She'd take their checks and dole out the money, usually spent in her bar, cafe and house, until there was none left. Then it was back to pushing cattle.

Today Lena is in her 80s, a strong, powerful figure yet. She stands about 5'7", her body thickening, but nowhere near fat, her hair, a half-hearted red tint partially covering the grey.

She and her friends have settled at a table in the back.

The bartender approaches her cautiously. He tells her there's a woman at the end of the bar who wants to talk to her about the Club Cigar.

Lena shifts her weight onto her feet, stands, then shuffles purposefully — with even a bit of grace — down to where I'm sitting. She extends a hand as gnarled as a limb of an old eastern Montana cottonwood.

Lena is nothing if not gracious. Someone wants to meet her, by gosh, they can meet her, but they'd better understand she doesn't have a whole lot of time or patience.

Some would call her face a horse face — long and broad, with features set close in to the middle. And it is that, but it also is a handsome face, distinctive in the off-pattern way of women with unusual, definitive looks.

She is the sort of woman any person with sense would never impose on. Having consciously developed the persistence and impertinence necessary in a journalistic career, I was pulled up short with Lena. The questions stacked up in my mind; tried to push out my mouth, but Lena was there. And she didn't have a lot of time. She was with her friends — old friends — and they always crossed the street about 10 and had dinner at Sambo's. She had come to oblige, to meet me, but beyond that I was on my own. All I could get out of Lena without stepping over that line she had so clearly drawn was that she had "taken care of everyone — all the cowhands."

Her voice was that of a chain smoker. There was hard living in it, but no age. She extended her hand again — what a hand — smooth, worn skin stretched over arthritic fingers, each

Outhouses at the Jersey Lilly

finger bent at a right angle on the last joint — a strong hand, with a hell of a grip yet.

John Tovson, who has leased the Club Cigar from Lena, has done a nice job of renovating the place. It's comfortable and clean and old without the presumptuous quality of overdone chic antique. (Still, it's changed a little too much for Lena. She does her drinking across the street at the Legion.)

The monolithic mahogany back bar, one of the most impressive in the state, dates back to 1904. An older oak back bar, previously used in the Club's cafe section, stands at a right angle to the larger back bar. Both bars have mirror backs. The mahogany stands in gleaming columns about 10 feet tall and extends some 20 feet. Its mirrored back reflects oak ceiling fans, old globe lights, a brass rail surrounding a raised seating section.

They've propped a large television screen at the end of the bar, but it is no distraction a few feet away in the seating area. Drinks are mixed well and moderately priced. John serves sandwiches and soup for lunch. What we have here is a fine old multi-purpose saloon with a rich past and a promising future. I recommend it on any tour of Great Falls.

John tells me the Ponderosa Motel on the end of the street bought up the land where the Mint Bar stood, that famous hangout of Charlie Russell.* The Ponderosa people destroyed the Mint for their chrome and vinyl motel, and John says they would have bought the Club Cigar if it weren't for Lena. Like I said, Lena is a formidable figure. She may eat at Sambo's, but she does business with them purely on her own terms.

---

*Actually, the Mint has come to be known as a Russell hangout because a collection of Russell paintings were moved to the Mint when the Silver Dollar (formerly across the street from the Mint) was closed for Prohibition. The Silver Dollar was owned by Billy Rance, long-time friend of Russell and was, at the time, his main watering hole.

The Midway
416 West Main
Lewistown

In the Midway I learn more about the bankrolling of ranch hands and sheepherders. Tony Geis has owned the Midway since 1946. Before that he owned the Glacier Bar in Great Falls and he built the Bar 19 in Lewistown.

He remembers the old days, when the hands would come in from the range: "They'd come in and cash a check. Then the bartender would parcel it out in 20s and 50s. The first thing they'd do is get a shave and a haircut. Then they'd go to Jason's and get a hat and a pair of boots. They'd always come in with a bedroll. In the case of a sheepherder, you always had their dog. The dog would lay under a table. Generally the boss knew how long it would take for them to spend their money."

Tony assures me Lena Ford was a main bankroller in Great Falls, adding it was her practice to fill a whiskey bottle with tea so she could drink all day with the boys. Tony remembers another bankrolling instance in a bar in Harlem: "A sheepherder drove up to this house and had $600. He was buying all the drinks. Everyone crowded around. A rancher came in and took the madam into the kitchen. He told her he definitely had to have the sheepherder back by Saturday — to make sure the guy's money was gone by then . . . . You could tell those guys they were broke in three days and they'd never know it."

The Midway sits behind a small mercantile that Tony established as a gourmet shop in the early days when he realized neither Billings nor Great Falls had a gourmet store. Now that both towns have their own outlets, Tony has shifted his stock to take-out liquor, basic grocery items, and odd, assorted merchandise, including wood-burning stoves.

The Midway is beyond the store. The bar is small, clean, orderly and dark in midday, with a fine old dark wood back bar inlaid with mirrors and stained glass, and booths for visiting. To the side of the bar is a Chinese restaurant Tony started in the early 1970s.

Tony has spent most of his life in a bar. During Prohibition he watched his father bootleg whiskey. He remembers when his father stored up 150 cases of whiskey. "He said he had enough to last the rest of his life," Tony remembers. "It was gone in three years."

Like Charley and Esther Judd, Sonny O'Day, Moose, Chuck Colier, Luigi, Trixie, and so many of the bartenders I've met on my search, Tony Geis is a pro. These pros are respected and revered as modern day storytellers, entertainers, purveyors of local legend, as well as important contemporary information sources. If you want to know something about an area, it is likely you will be sent to one of these men or women.

You rarely will see them take a drink. Most of them will sit and drink coffee and tell you stories for about as long as you can listen. My friend, Kate, and I sat with Tony one early hungover Sunday afternoon and listened to story after story.

Just about anything goes with these bartenders — in their business and in their tolerance of the human condition. You will see every sort of person in their bars. And you will see them treat these very different people with equal respect and hospitality. You rarely will see any trouble. If there is a fight, their customers often will take care of the disturbance. Most of them are at least relatively wealthy. They are astute business people. They will try to sell you anything.

Take Tony Geis — with his shrimp, fried rice and egg rolls, his wood-burning stoves, imported olives, and take-out wine. (Actually, there is an affinity between Chinese food and Montana bars. Old-timers will tell you that in the early days in the bigger towns in the state, every other door on a busy street was a bar, and the doors in between were Chinese restaurants.)

Tony grew up in Great Falls. He remembers playing with Charlie Russell's stepson as a young boy: "I used to beat up the stepson," Tony says with a grin. "Then one of us would cry and he'd (Russell) call us into the cabin where they lived, and he'd talk to us, and then hand us a horse or a cow that he'd formed out of clay while he was talking to us."

Another story I liked was about Lewistown's resident bank robber. Tony claims the man (who will go unnamed here) was active in the area in the 1960s, but hasn't robbed a bank in Montana for years. "They say he's robbin' them in the Midwest," Tony says. He claims the man, a friend of his, brought his take into the Midway a couple of times. The first time, Tony says, "he spilled money up and down the bar. There were thousands in cash. I asked him where he got the money. He said his mother just died and he inherited it."

Not long after that the man came in again. This time he had a bag of money and it was sopping wet. The money was wet, Tony tells me, because the robber had to run water into the safe as he was cutting through the lock. The torch would have burned through to the paper money.

"Got a place where I can dry out some money?" the robber asked Tony. "Did your mother die again?" Tony wanted to know. But he did let the guy spread out the money to dry in the bar's basement.

Missoula and Ovando

Missoula Club

139 W. Main

Missoula

One of the most treasured services a bar can offer, at least for me, is a grill-fried burger. That's part of the reason I find the Missoula Club so worthwhile. The Club serves one of the best burgers you're likely to find in this century.

Fried right in front of your very eyes, spitting little wads of grease up toward the fan, creamy juice onto the grill. Your nose pulls in the thick, pungent aroma of frying meat. You long for that first warm, wet, absolutely satiating bite.

The bartender flips the patty and then firmly presses it onto the grill. Minutes are hours. You're sure you haven't eaten in years.

The bartender presses it one more time; then pulls if off the grill. He sets it on a golden toasted bun and then onto the plate. A little catsup, a touch of mustard, you cap it with the bun and close your eyes as you lift it to your lips. You bite through the just-crisp bun, into the slice of raw — so sharp, so ripe, so Onion — and then to the Monterey jack cheese — deep and soothing — a pleasant forerunner to what comes next — the richly complex flavor of beef.

Whip me; beat me; make me sit behind the five-way intersection at Russell and South for three light changes, but when I come to Missoula let me eat a burger at the Missoula Club.

People who don't drink beat down the Missoula Club's door for the burgers — and what's more — they chill their beer glasses. A draft sipped from a frosted mug, any beer drinker knows, is ever so much more pleasant than one pulled down at common room temperature.

The Missoula Club has never been a club. The closest it's come to a club is when people were first getting television sets. On New Year's day and on special occasions — namely the Bowl Games — certain people were allowed through the door to watch the games.

It's always been a sport bar — baseball mainly — but the rest of them have their share of attention. Pennants and pictures of just about every team ever organized in Missoula constitute the decor.

The Missoula Club's front seems nothing more than that of an old cigar store, and really, the bar — outside of the burgers and the general ambience — is about that. A lot of old men, but young ones too, and couples, businessmen, jocks, college students.

The back bar is old mahogany that's seen better days, with matching plank and plastic covered stools pulled up close. It's a straight shot to the back. People often catch baseball or football games on television at the end of the bar while they watch their burgers fry.

For years there was a small gymnasium below the Missoula Club where fighters would train. Joe Dugle, owner of the Club the last seven years, said Ford Smith, who was the first of 10 ranked heavy weights in 1936, trained in the gym. Henry Armstrong who held three titles at one time, also trained there. Armstrong lost to Richie Fontaine. Dugle said Smith fought Buddy Baer for the heavy weight title. He said the match paid the highest amount to that date on a preliminary fight — $55,000.

He couldn't remember who won. I don't really care who won, but I can't help but wonder how Armstrong and Smith could stay in training with the burgers frying upstairs.

Silver Dollar Bar

307 West Railroad
Missoula

Most of the bars in Missoula after Prohibition were near the railroad tracks on Railroad and Woody streets. I'm in the Silver Dollar, talking to Bill Morgan, who once delivered papers in the area. He is telling me there once were 14 bars on a few blocks of Woody and Railroad. The railroad served as the main artery of the town then, and a good part of Missoula's business centered around it.

Bill can name off just about every bar in existence then — D'Orazi's, Spider Maverick's, the Brunswick, the Keith Hotel, the Garden City One and Two, the Sunshine, the Atlantic, the Bar of Justice. Many of them had accompanying houses of prostitution.

Now the Silver Dollar, a clean but worn survivor of more vibrant days, attracts railroaders off shift, old-timers of the area, rugby players, and young people searching out the rougher side of Missoula night life.

Bill Morgan is telling me about an old bartender who frequents the Silver Dollar. He had worked at the Garden City bar for years and had been married to a woman who was called the *Witch of Woody Street*. A few minutes later, the old bartender comes in. He tells me he and the Witch had worked together as bartender and bouncer.

"Who was the bouncer?" I ask.

"She was," he replies, his eyebrows arched. His look blends respect with loathing.

"Was she that tough?" I ask.

"She didn't take no shit," he mumbles and orders another straight shot.

o—O—o

Missoula is a good bar town — from the old man's all night **Oxford, Inc.,** 337 N. Higgins, to the decadent singles' druggedness of the **Top Hat,** 134 W. Front. The Oxford's breakfasts are famous among all age groups and the Top Hat is known throughout the state for various reasons, a main one being the fine bluegrass and jazz bands it books. The **Stockman's,** 125 W. Front, with its large cafe counter, liquor store, bar and poker room, is a well-loved all-purpose bar.

The Flame, 122 W. Main, is a garishly stylistic old cocktail lounge. Its rosy backlighted glow and plush half-moon booths offer a relaxing haven from reality. **Red's Bar,** 217 Ryman is a great old baseball bar that never changes and has outlived numerous other bars on the same street. The **Elbow Room,** 1025 Strand, is an affable working man's bar. **The Shack,** 223 W. Front, not long ago a greasy chicken cafe, now, with its stuccoed walls, posters and knotty pine is a refreshing spot for a beer and a sandwich. **Luke's Bar,** 231 W. Front, a young people's bar that features local musicians, has the impressive collection of Lee Nye's old-timer's photos that once hung in Eddy's Club.

Trixie's Antler Saloon
Highway 200
Ovando

WARNING — THIS PROPERTY PROTECTED BY ARMED CITIZEN. Welcome to Trixie's Antler Saloon, showplace of one of the country's first women trick ropers, and home of the best in antique western funk. A bullet hole in the ceiling above the bar pays tribute to Trixie's theme — the West's highly-prized, zealously-protected RIGHT TO KEEP AND BEAR ARMS.

"He was just playing," Trixie will explain to me later. The signs are everywhere: ANTI-GUN IS ANTI-AMERICAN, they shout. ENDANGERED SPECIES — FIREARMS & FREEDOM, they reiterate.

Trixie, one of the most renowned bartenders in western Montana, sold the bar to Leo Bush more than a year ago. She ran the saloon more than 18 years — an appropriate cap to a 20-year stint in show business — and then retired to her hometown, Hamilton.

I talked with Trixie over the telephone a few months after visiting her saloon. She told me she had been drawn to trick roping when she was 15 years old. Bob Rooker, a famous trick roper, told her there weren't many women who could trick rope, and it might be a good gig for her.

Trixie needed no more encouragement. She began to work with the rope. She practiced her way into fairs and rodeos, then to a vaudeville act, a U.S.O. show in Mexico City, to Australia, the Cow Palace in San Francisco, then television. "You Asked for It" asked for Trixie. Then she did stunts in the movies.

Trixie not only threw a mean rope, she did it off the back of a horse. But 20 years were enough for Trixie. She retired from show business while she was still young and leased a saloon in Ovando. She ran that bar for a few years and then bought another liquor license for this saloon a mile east of town.

The Wan-I-Gan in the Paradise Valley

Trixie gathered all kinds of antiques and oddities over the years she had the bar. Many of the strangest pieces were brought in by customers who wanted them preserved for posterity. There's a gnarled old pump organ and bench, a washtub and wringer, old paintings in gilded frames, Anheuser Busch girls in hand crafted pine frames, a couch covered in red imitation leather with a canopy fitted over it to make a hybrid couch/covered wagon, the head of a moose who looks to be kin of Bullwinkle, a stuffed iguana, old pine wood stools at the bar — one with a saddle for a seat, another with an old metal tractor seat — sheepshears, rusty with age, colorful Mexican cloth curtains.

You'll probably notice something new every time you stop in. The building housing the saloon was once an office building at Fort Harrison in Helena. To the side of the bar is a room — not more than a lean-to — with funky old tables, benches and chairs, and assorted antiques.

Trixie's is the only bar and only restaurant near Ovando. Actually, it's the only eating and/or drinking establishment in about a 20-mile radius. The locals make good use of the place; others travel out of their way to see it. Trixie's even without the aging trick roper, is still one of Montana's more celebrated saloons.

The food is adequate, if not notable — the basics in sandwiches, soups, chicken, steaks. If you live around Ovando it's the only alternative to home cooking. Helen Bush says she and her husband get about as much business as they can handle. "Hayers come in — there will be 18 or 19 of them," she says, "but if you've got other people in here, they're good. They just sit and have a few drinks."

Flathead and the Yaak

Dirty Shame Saloon

Yaak River Road
Yaak

I'm on my way to the infamous Dirty Shame Saloon, a bar that caters to a sparse 150 people in about that many square miles of wild backwoods in the northwest corner of the state. I'd been to the Yaak one time before, driving the relatively modern road up from Libby. This time I'm taking the northern route through Eureka, over the Purcell range to the Yaak, some of the most beautifully untamed country in the state.

I stop in the Eureka Bar and talk with a few young Forest Service workers beginning their weekend this late Friday afternoon. The Eureka is dark and slow, even on a fast day. It seems slow, not because business is off, but because no one is in the slightest hurry. I think an elk could walk in and die on the middle of the dance floor and no head would turn. The weekend is serious business in Eureka.

One young man tells me he likes the Eureka Bar because that's where his friends meet. Across the street is the Stockman's where the gyppo loggers drink. The guy says he's heard a lot of bad about the gyppos, but any of them he has met in the woods have been fine people. Still, he'd just as soon drink in the Eureka. Later, a logger will classify Forest Service workers as "educated idiots." I decide it might be best in Eureka for the Forest Service to stay on one side of the street, and leave the other to the gyppos.

On the way out of town I stop for one for the road at a small grocery store. I'm told how to get to the Yaak and that I'm crazy if I go alone at night. The road is bad, they say, and there's no one to help if you break down, but I decide to chance it.

A few miles out of town I take the wrong turn. It takes me about an hour and a half to correct the error and by this time I'm on a hiking trail the map shows as a paved road, climbing a mountain pass. (Later, I learn the road was put in by a New Deal crew and remains historically accurate.)

Two hours later I stumble weak-kneed into the Dirty Shame. Hasn't changed a bit. The same wood-planked front porch, the same deer rack used as a door handle, the battered pool table, the loose bathroom door, the grotesque graffiti inside, the loggers, ranchers, recreationists, Forest Service people, using the bar like a third leg, a poker game in the corner, a huge wood burner in another.

The Dirty Shame is the fresh, sharp smell of pine, and the dank odor of dirt-laden, beer-splashed floors, wild nights of revelry, and mornings of shared pain.

Irascible, strong-willed, folksy, accommodating, the Dirty Shame is as honest a bar as you'll ever find.

It even came by its name honestly. The story begins with an air force base that was located in the Yaak in the early 1950s. Our narrator is Glenn Johnson, a compassionate, rotund logger/bartender, well respected in the Yaak, a patron of the Dirty Shame going on two decades.

Glenn tells me, a man by the name of Kennedy saw the air force base go in, bought a beer license, hauled beer up from Libby and set up business in a shack, grandly naming the place the Yaak River Lodge.

The air force men manning a D.E.W. (Distant Early Warning) system had lived many places, but never in the Yaak. They drank at the Yaak River Lodge, but they didn't like it; most of them choked on the name. "It was a shack, and it was dirty," Glenn remembers. Eventually Kennedy got a liquor license, but the place didn't get any cleaner. The men from the base would come and drink because there was no place else within 40 miles. They'd look around and then mumble to each other, "Now, isn't this a dirty shame?" The grandly named Yaak River Lodge never really had a chance.

Glenn tells me the present Dirty Shame is the result of

seven shacks pushed together in one way or another. He's helped with the redecorating through the years.

Glenn tells me many stories over the three hours I spend with him and other Dirty Shame patrons. He'd cut off my arm at the elbow before he'd let me buy a beer. My favorite story is about a few Yaak residents, free-roaming cows, tourists and law enforcement. Glenn begins the story with an explanation. "In most places, you got to fence cows in; here ya got to fence 'em out."

The story: A man named Jimmy had a trailer a couple of hundred feet from the Dirty Shame. Another area resident had a herd of cattle that grazed a broad area over the summer. A few of them were showing a real affinity for Jimmy's trailer. Jimmy claimed the cattle would come into his yard, stomp bicycle tires, and shake his trailer when they rubbed against it. Jimmy told people in the Dirty Shame one night, "I'm getting damned tired of those cows rubbing on my trailer and [me] walking home drunk every night through the shit . . . ." He warned the rancher to keep the cattle out of his yard.

One afternoon Jimmy was shooting pool in the Dirty Shame when another local walked into the bar and told him the cattle were in his yard again. Jimmy didn't hesitate. He handed the pool cue to a friend standing nearby, picked up the rifle he had kept with him for just this purpose, walked a few steps out of the Dirty Shame and plugged some seven cows. Then he walked back into the bar and shot the four ball into the corner pocket.

The cattle lay dead on the road.

Later in the afternoon, another local showed up at the Dirty Shame. He wanted to know what had happened. He said tourists passing through kept asking him what all the dead cows were doing on the road.

It didn't take the law officers long to catch up with Jimmy, considering there are no law officers within about 40 miles of the Yaak. "They grabbed Jimmy and put him in jail," Glenn says. "A lot of women around here were pretty upset about it. They went into the jail with six-packs — gonna camp in there til they got him out." Finally Jimmy was released with a $250 fine. Glenn thought it was a pretty good deal for everyone involved.

There are many things that distinguish the Yaak and the Dirty Shame from most of Montana and the country. For instance, everyone in the area burns wood. Electricity has come to the Yaak, but forget about natural gas. Locating, cutting and storing wood for the winter consumes a good part of summer and fall free time. Another interesting aspect of

Yaak living is the rural community ethic, which translates into: Everyone knows everyone else's business; everyone is taken care of. "All the major decisions are made here," Glenn laughs.

The night I was in the Dirty Shame the widow of a man shot and killed two days before in an ugly incident was in the bar with several friends. When she left, Glenn told me they were planning a benefit dance for her and planned to "set her up with wood for the winter." The woman runs another bar in the area and she burns about 25 cords of wood a year.

Glenn lists off several other benefits organized for people down on their luck. Besides benefits, the Dirty Shame is big on dances. Usually on weekends they have local musicians play: "Hundreds and hundreds of dances," Glenn says. "No one stays home in the winter," he adds. Everyone hangs out at the Dirty Shame and makes full use of the wood cut for the bar.

Owning a CB is vital in the Yaak. "Everyone gets on the CBs," Glenn says. "One person will be going to Libby or Spokane for groceries. They'll get on the CB and take orders and get groceries for 10 families." The Yaak's remoteness makes for added expenses for locals and tourists alike. You'll pay $2.50 for a hamburger in the Dirty Shame, but you can buy a dozen fresh eggs any day of the week for seventy cents.

Staying in line in the Yaak is a good idea: "Someone gets out of line and everyone knows it in five minutes," Glenn laughs. "It's fun. We don't have T.V. here . . . ."

A couple of guys in the Yaak are renowned moonshiners, possibly a cultural holdover from Prohibition days when the traffic of Canadian whiskey was heavy in many Montana border towns. Glenn lists off the liquors made by these men: brandy, whiskey, cognac, gin, and adds, "Every once in a while they make a cup of coffee."

Moose's Saloon
Main Street
Kalispell

At first glance Moose's Saloon seems like any other sawdust-floored young people's beer pub. Cutely inscribed T-shirts and baseball caps are the uniform. At 9:30 on a Tuesday night the place is packed. Coming from a quiet dinner and several cups of coffee, a walk into Moose's is like opening the door to an eighth grade study hall.

A hefty mug of cold beer later, the picture changes. I'm talking to Moose — about 6'3", 220 pounds of intelligence and good nature. Moose was a defensive tackle for the University of Montana Grizzlies in younger days. He was all set with teaching credentials in 1957 when his wife inherited the Corral Bar from her father.

They came to Kalispell, where they found the Corral — "four bare plywood walls, two flourescent lights, no business and a $10,000 mortgage." What followed is a fine case history in business success. Moose has expanded the place twice. Besides the large rectangular bar, the saloon has an area the size of a large dance floor filled with booths and picnic tables,

and absolutely packed with people. The three hours I'm there I don't see a let-up in the flow of beer.

Moose talks to me as he washes pitchers. He says he's been lucky — got some breaks, some good press. He points to a story about Evel Knievel that appeared in *Sports Illustrated.* Evel supposedly concocted the Idaho Falls jump while drinking in Moose's Saloon.

Drinking what he (apparently no one else) calls Montana Mary's (red beer), Evel told the writer of the article, Robert F. Jones, he decided he could jump the Grand Canyon while studying a photo of it in Moose's. "The more I studied on it and the more Montana Mary's I put back, the narrower that durned hole in the ground seemed to get . . . . People talk about the generation gap and the missile gap and the education gap, but I suddenly saw that the real gap was right out there in the heart of the Golden West. And I knew I could bridge the bastard . . . ."

As the night wears on I know the key to Moose's success has little to do with an article in *Sports Illustrated.* Everyone in the place seems to know him, at least well enough to call out a greeting. Moose functions as friend/confessor/beneficent curer of ills. As we talk about bars and the strange and funny incidents Moose has witnessed, he becomes concerned that I don't miss one aspect of what it is to own a bar.

He tells me about Jack McCarthy, who for years owned a bar in Kalispell. Jack cared about people, Moose says. He cared about dogs. He'd take stray dogs and find them a home. He fed birds. And he buried anyone that didn't have a family to bury them.

"Jack was in the bar business all his life," Moose goes on. "He was the epitome of what a bar owner should be. How many guys do you know that would bury people? You have to actually have an attachment, a feeling for the people. A bartender should give you what you came in for. Too many people just throw you a drink."

While we're talking a man in his mid-30s with a round middle and hearty voice comes to the bar, obviously excited to see Moose. He's a Shakespearean actor, Moose tells me when the man has settled with his pitcher of beer and his friends. The actor grew up in a small town in Montana, but lives in Chicago now. He spent a summer in Kalispell conducting Shakespearean workshops. He wants to come back for a summer and do it again. Moose tells me the man does a great Othello.

The actor is back. While he talks to Moose I take a walk around the bar. Moose is a junk collector, he has told me. His "junk" is a fine selection of beer trays, opium pipes, Sullivan-esque paintings in rich, gilded frames, a framed letter from the manager of a Wild West show telling "How Tom Mix's Wild West Show was Stoned Out of Butte," and another framed document — an "Invitation to an Execution." Above the beautiful old National cash register are several dollar bills tacked on thick planks. Moose says people tack a dollar with their name on it to the wood so they've always got another beer coming.

A friendly young Canadian I had talked to earlier comes and pulls up a stool next to me. After a brief chat about how expensive it is to live in Canada these days, the traveling electrician is ready to take his leave. I put out my hand for a goodbye shake and the guy, whose speech seems a blend of French-Canadian and North Dakota-ese tells me he's traveled through a good part of Europe, through most of the States and into South America, etc. And nowhere has he seen women offer their hands to shake like they do in Montana.

Moose is back washing pitchers. He has a few good stories about bars, most of them unprintable. One morning he came in and found footprints all over the bar plank. He asked the night bartender what had happened. The guy said, "Ah Moose, you shoulda been here," and then went on to describe the striptease.

The Blue Moon
On Highway 93
South of Columbia Falls

The owners of the Blue Moon claim the longest bar in the Northwest — "at least 60 feet if you straighten it out" — but have had what might be called a pissing contest with bar owners in Washington state about the same issue. Anyway, it is a long bar.

The Blue Moon is very dark, cheap and funky. Its main decorating scheme consists of three-foot stripes of gawdy red, white and blue vinyl. The vinyl was painted for the BiCentennial and hasn't been changed. It's the kind of bar that creates an atmosphere by default. Very little is done for effect; therein lies the effect. Everytime I've been in the Blue Moon (stopping in randomly for close to 10 years), I've felt it a choice hiding spot. It seems to exist outside the normal pattern of things, an archetypal good time bar.

Dick and Charlotte Sapa own the place. They live in an apartment next to the bar with their three children.

They acquired the Blue Moon on a sealed bid about seven years ago, largely because Dick is a musician and he saw owning a bar as a way to combine music, business and family life. A bandstand stretches across the side of the large room; chairs and tables fill up space below it. There's plenty of room for dancing. Dick and his band play a wild country western rock six nights a week, contributing to the Blue Moon's reputation as a bar where every night is Saturday night and every Saturday night is New Year's Eve.

The Sapas and a friend are bantering over some color photos the afternoon I stop in. I drink a couple of beers with them. It soon becomes clear the Sapas believe in a close association with the community. The bar's their home; customers are friends and neighbors. Charlotte calls it being friendly. She says they have been rewarded many times over for any good they've done.

One afternoon, Charlotte remembers, soon after they had bought the Blue Moon, a young man was bragging about the horse he had just acquired. He told Charlotte he wanted to bring the horse over to show it off. Charlotte said, fine. (She tells me she didn't want to discourage business.) Sure enough, the guy goes and gets the horse and rides it into the bar. He orders a ditch for himself and a gin and tonic for the horse. Horses are supposed to like gin, Charlotte explains.

The horse did slurp a little of the drink, but Charlotte says, "he spilled as much as he drank." Sloppy horse. Crude, too. On the way out he lifted his tail and . . . . Dick and Charlotte argue over who cleaned up the mess.

The Sapas usually are involved in community benefits of one kind or another. The big deal is Memorial Day, when they host Columbia Falls and anyone else in the general vicinity to a pig roast — 250 pounds of pork roasted 24 hours on a spit, 100 pounds of potato salad, 30 pounds of baked beans, keg beer, a horseshoe tournament, baseball games.

Soon Dick is talking with another customer. Charlotte and I discuss what it is to own a bar. People like to know the bartender, she tells me — they like to come in and know there is someone to talk to.

An hour later I'm about to leave. A young man comes in, a friend of Charlotte's. He tells her he's got the baby out in the car. Charlotte and I walk out to the car with the guy. As I pull out of the parking lot Charlotte is cooing over the baby.

Along The Yellowstone

The New Atlas

528 Pike Avenue
Columbus

The day is golden red Indian summer. The sky is turquoise. The temperature is in the 70s. My search for the perfect Montana bar goes happily east of the Rockies. The New Atlas in Columbus is my first planned stop. Today the Atlas is a little crowded, a little rowdy, but friendly, too, even polite.

Bartender Kenny has the lid on, but he's still doing a good business this Tuesday afternoon. A large back room holds a poker game, lively at three thirty. The long bar is packed with people and an impressive collection of stuffed birds and animals.

Hulking throughout the room are bald eagles, an albino mule deer fawn, a coyote howling to the moon, young bobcats fighting, an Audak (African mountain sheep), a Canadian lynx, a raccoon or two, a fox, a snow owl, moose heads, elk heads — buffalo, antelope, mountain sheep — all kinds of heads — a two-headed calf — deformed racks, other aberrations of the animal world.

The bar is so full of people, animals and birds I have to stand to have a drink. The back bar, a beautiful mahogany reminiscent of the former Turf in Missoula and Great Falls' Club Cigar, dates back to 1906. Another back bar — mirrored, like the main bar — sits opposite the mahogany plank. Sitting at the bar you can see yourself coming and going in the mirrors of the two bars. You can also see dual reflections of all the animals, mounted heads, antlers, etc., and after a few drinks they seem to be coming and going, too.

Above is the decorative pressed tin ceiling found in most old Montana bars. Spittoons built into the bar's footrest and square dark wood booths also date the place. A large selection of paperback books sits opposite the back bar. The books rest on an old glass and oak display counter which is filled with assorted miscellany, most of it junk. An old unplugged television set acts as a bookend for the paperback collection.

Bartender Kenny, whose starched white shirt fails to cover a tattoo above his wrist, says the paperbacks sell for fifty cents and you get a quarter if you bring them back. An ornately carved old upright piano commands proper attention in the middle of the large room. A mug of draft beer is as cheap as in Butte, thirty-five cents. "When I Get Over You" is on the jukebox.

The clientele is the mix found often in good old-time bars. Much of the conversation is between people who have known each other for so long they hardly look at one another when they talk. Their words are spaced with long, thoughtful silences — the conversation of people who have lived, worked and drunk together for decades in a town no more than a square mile in size.

There are a few old drunks and a friendly middle-aged bartender from Reedpoint who urges me to stop at the bar where he works. Young geologists who hail from back East are in for a drink before going out to work the night shift. They're looking for uranium around Columbus, working 12 to 14 hours a day, everyday.

When they have left for work I look around and see the bar has cleared.

Now, here's an authentic all-purpose, old-time bar — one that's busy at three-thirty, nearly empty at five. It's Kenny, the animals and birds, poker players in the back, a couple of old guys and me.

There's a queer sensation that goes with drinking surrounded by dead, stuffed animals. The first reaction is one of nonchalance — ah some nice stuffed animals. After a few drinks you feel countless pairs of eyes bearing down. You have another beer to relax under the scrutiny, look around again, and you're among friends, the animals' glares having softened to amused acceptance.

I have another draft. The old drunk next to me is making no sense at all. That's O.K., because by now I'm enjoying the coming and going in the mirrors. Kenny comes back with a smile and my change. Silver dollars. Real money. I know I've crossed the Rockies now.

My pockets heavy again, it's time to push on. On to Billings and Forsyth and Miles City and Ingomar and Ekalaka, and perhaps Two Dot, through the sun and dust and roll of the Yellowstone River Valley.

Waterhole Saloon
Reed Point

While Columbus' New Atlas may well be the best taxidermy bar in Montana, neighboring Reed Point's Waterhole Saloon is making a go for the best zoo bar. "We've had just about every kind of animal in here," says owner Chris Hahn — "goats, ducks, sheep, horses, owls. A couple of weeks ago I had to kill a bat that was dive-bombing the bar."

Until a few weeks before my visit, Otis, the pig had been the star of the show. Chris bought Otis from a guy passing through Reed Point. He paid two shots of whiskey and a Waterhole bumper sticker.

Otis was cute then, only two weeks old. "He was raised in the bar," Chris tells me. "He ate peanuts and drank beer. He was drunk all the time. He'd shell the peanuts out and eat 'em."

The next question, obviously, is where is Otis now?

"He's been eaten," Chris says, with the nonchalance of a well-fed carnivore. "Wasn't worth a damn to eat. Really bad. We took 75 pounds of lard out of him — all that beer and peanuts."

But, if he wasn't much of a ham dead, Otis was entertaining while alive. Chris tells how Otis would play with the dogs in Reed Point: "He'd run up and down Main Street. He'd chase the dogs; then they'd chase him." Chris shows me pictures of Otis at the bar, adding "they're a better pet than a dog."

I'm wondering — since Otis was such a good pet — why they didn't keep him around a while longer. My question is answered when I ask if Otis still lived in the bar after he was fully grown. "When they're 400 pounds," Chris says, "it's hard to keep 'em out."

Chris Hahn built the Waterhole Saloon about five years ago. It's a fine replica of an old saloon, all done in wood by Hahn and a few helpers. The front is decked with a wood plank sidewalk, much like the front of the Jersey Lilly in Ingomar. Chris tells me he was thinking of the Jersey Lilly when he built the Waterhole. The Jersey Lil was his idea of a classic Montana saloon.

Inside is a haven of wood — ponderosa pine, juniper, redwood, oak — all kinds of wood, worked into bar stools, chairs, tables, the plank and back bar. And the smell is wood, from the old school house stove that heats the large room.

The back bar is made from old fence posts, the plank from pine. Drawers worked into the back bar are made of oak dowels, remnants of a cradle manufacturing business that operated in Reed Point in the early 1960s.

Chris bought the building, gutted it out, then took the better part of a year to rebuild his bar and a steakhouse in the back. Business has been down, so the steakhouse is closed the day I stop in.

It's a cool fall day, early afternoon. The Waterhole is full of hunters, locals and ranchers. Most of them are drinking whiskey. One local comes in, announcing, "finally captured one." Someone asks what the guy got.

"A four point," he sighs. "Tried to get a bigger one, but he wouldn't slow down long enough."

Chris is telling me Reed Point, now a town of less than 100 population, was once the biggest town on the Yellowstone — before either Billings or Livingston became established. Chris had found a Reed Point paper from 1916 that listed several banks, lumber yards, and five or six saloons. "We had our own dentists, doctors, attorneys," Chris tells me, obviously impressed. "It was quite the place."

"Reed Point died," Chris says, "and now it's on the rejuvenation list. People are moving here from all over the U.S." I ask why. "They're coming mainly from the city," Chris says. "They're after a life style."

About this time a rough-looking, but friendly customer

approaches the bar. "Give me a bottle of Black Velvet and a case of pop," he says. Another customer asks the guy where he's going.

"Goin' out to set coyote traps," the guy says, a confident gleam in his eye. I wonder if the newcomers to Reed Point are ready for this much life style.

Sonny O'Day's Bar & Lounge
Main Street
Laurel

I hadn't planned to stop in Laurel on this trip. Coming back from Red Lodge, I was just about to take the Interstate ramp to Billings when a bar mentioned by people in my travels surfaced in my mind.

Sonny something, I think, yeah, and he's in Laurel. Charley Judd of Butte's New Deal had mentioned him; years ago it seemed my father had talked about him; a few acquaintances along the road had referred to him, but I'm having trouble getting a focus. Anyway, I steer past the ramp and into downtown Laurel.

Sure enough, there on Main is a bar with a Sonny O'Day sign. I park the little Renault and open the door to Sonny O'Day's. I'm greeted promptly, aggressively. His speech is unmistakably Butte — Brooklyn once removed.

"Where's your old man?" is the first thing. "Don't have one," is the reply. That bothers him. "Where ya from?" Almost before I reply he asks, "Who's your family?" I tell him. He's delighted. He knows my family.

Now I remember. Sonny O'Day is the boxer who runs a bar in Laurel and is a stronghold in eastern Montana Democratic politics. A look around his place tells the story: Democrats and boxers all over the place, and a painting of Sonny in younger days standing by the Savoy in what was once Meaderville, Butte.

At the end of the bar a life-size photo of Sonny in boxing shorts is stretched from ceiling to below bar level. It was probably taken before his 21st birthday. It is a photo of a beautiful, smooth-bodied, strong-faced young man bent gracefully at the waist, a determined glare on his face, dukes up for the camera.

I begin the usual bombardment of questions, but Sonny has a mile lead. (An article that appeared in the Billings Gazette mentioned his rapid speech and others I will talk to later about Sonny are quick to laugh about how fast he talks.)

Sonny takes my hand and leads me around his establishment, which he calls a boxing museum. Calling me *darlink and babee* and swooping up my hand should he lose it as he darts from here to there, he shows me his collection of photos and with that breathless speech tells the story behind each.

He *does* have a collection of photos. He claims there are 1,000 fighters, all the photos personally autographed; 67 world champions, 11 photographed with Sonny behind the bar.

There's Rocky Marciano, Floyd Patterson, and a photo of the first legal fight on the Pacific Coast, at Colma, Calif., in 1905. There's Mose LaFonsie and the original Dixie Kid — bare knuckles in Boulder, Montana, 25 rounds. There's "Sugar" Ray Robinson, Sonny Liston, and Sonny's prize promotion, a middleweight championship fight between Joey

Giardello and Gene Fulmer in Bozeman in 1960. Sonny called it a draw.

There are Butte boxers — the Michigan Assassin and Montana Jack Sullivan. There were five world champions living in Butte shortly after the turn of the century, Sonny says. There's John L. "Slug 'Em" Sullivan and Primo Carnera. There's Jack Dempsey tending bar with Sonny.

One of my favorites is behind the bar — Charlie Russell posed with Jack Dempsey. And there's Cassius Clay sitting in what was once a training room, now opened up and part of the bar. He was sitting right here, says Sonny, pointing to a built up section in the old run-down former training room. Sure enough, the picture reflects the spot. I'm fascinated by the idea that Ali paid a visit to Sonny before he made it big. But Sonny is not too impressed with Ali, or maybe he's in a hurry to show me more. Here's Nat Fleischer, the father of boxing. He takes me to his safe and shows me more. He says his bar is nationally famous as a boxing museum, a home of champions.

But more interesting than all the photos on his wall is Sonny, himself. What is a guy so obviously *Butte* doing in Laurel? Sonny takes me around the story a few different routes over the hours I spend with him. Here's the gist: forget the Irish of his name, Sonny is as Italian as fettucini. Charles George is his given name. Charles George was 10, a punk in Butte with a paper route when promoters spotted him in an altercation. Shortly thereafter, he fought in the 100-pound

The New Atlas in Columbus

division in a boxing-crazed Butte. The promoters gave him a new name, so his father — recovering from a World War I wound in Fort Harrison — wouldn't know his son was boxing. They spelled it Sunny O'Dea.

A few years later Sonny's father was still ailing and wanted to return to his birthplace, Lucca, Italy. Sonny accompanied him to Italy. From there he boxed in North Africa, Hungary, Italy and Spain.

"I was an orphan at 14 years of age," Sonny tells me. "I had to fight to live." By the time he was 16, he was a professional boxer, a ham-n-egger, he says. He was a welter-weight. His strength was in his left. Only the managers made money on boxing in those days, Sonny tells me. His manager was a gambler. Sonny fought 529 fights and retired to Butte in 1938. He got a job as a bouncer at a place called the Rocky Mountain Cafe in Meaderville. Then he bought into the Savoy, one of Meaderville's choice joints, as he describes it, "One a da girlie joints, ya know — bootleggin, back in da turdies, in da Depression."

He began to build what he called a financial empire. Then came World War II. Sonny was gone for six years — in that time he claimed an army title — and when he returned to Butte he found his financial empire had dribbled to nothing. He lost the Savoy and another bar he owned — the Melody Lane — burned to the ground.

With the usual Butte-bred irony, Sonny says, "Dat town cost me two-hundret an seventy-seven tousant dollars — it took everting I had." The next minute he is calling Butte *his town*. A few minutes later he calls it the Sacred City, the last title I would have expected for Butte. Why, I ask. "Tree Catholic bishops" were born in Butte, he tells me, "dat's why."

After he lost the Melody Lane, Sonny landed in Billings, where he worked in a bar for a time. Then the bar owner set him up with a place in Laurel.

Sonny's made a good living at the bar, but to hear him talk, it's only a sideline to his ongoing boxing career. He continues on the state's boxing commission (an appointed position; no doubt a good part of the reason for all the politicians' photos in the bar) and is working on a book on boxing. He stays on top of the sport that he calls with reverence "the manly art of self-defense." Today he's taking the bus to Butte to check up on a fight he suspects was not entirely aboveboard.

I have to get back on the road, too, but first, I say, I want to take your picture. Sure, he says. Out in front of his bar, an opulent October sun drenching us in its descent, Sonny makes me pose with him in the same stance so many politicians and fighters have assumed for pictures with him — legs angled, about 18 inches apart, knuckles tight, dukes up — hold for the camera. Sonny positions his dukes and my dukes so he's got the inside with his famous left. Then he enlists an old man passing on the street to take the photo.

A few minutes later I'm on my way out the door of the bar. Sonny says, here, take a few beers wid ya. Nah, I say, that's okay. Oh yeah, he says. Well, maybe one for the road, I say. Sonny is back behind the bar. He's got a grocery bag and he is filling it.

No, Sonny, I say, just a beer for the road. He's getting beer, potato chips, gum, candy, popcorn, pretzels, beer nuts, and dumping it all into a big grocery sack. When I protest, he says, "You're on da road, ain't ya?" A few minutes later I'm walking out the door looking like I just did a week's shopping.

Sonny is worried I don't have enough to eat. He asks me if I like Reese candy bars. I've seen him throw at least three Reeses into the sack. I say, yeah, sure, thinking that will please him. He runs back and gets me a couple more. "Reeses are good for ya, ya know — dere not fattening."

He walks me over to the Renault, talking more about Lucca, Italy, his birthplace. He's planning a trip to Lucca. A minute later we're driving over to his house to seek a book on Lucca. There he gives me a sack of Macintosh apples.

The Seventeen Bar
1123 First Avenue North
Billings

The Seventeen Bar is one of the best testimonials I can name to the Montana work hard/play hard ethic: good food, good drink, good honky-tonk music.

Sitting on Billings' old main thoroughfare, left in the lurch with the routing of Interstate 90, the Seventeen still has the bustling stockyards across the street, a few good and cheap beef restaurants around it, and the fairgrounds to the east. It draws a clientele from at least an 80-mile radius — Roberts, Roundup, Huntley Project, Joliet, Hardin, Custer, Columbus — pulling the folks off the southeastern plains, up from the gullies, out from the sandstone silhouettes, rocky river beds and buttes.

The place is huge. I counted three bars. There's a dining area squared off from the bar, something like an indoor corral, pool and cards in the back, and a large dance floor, with seating scattered throughout.

The Seventeen is the epitome, if not an exaggeration, of the true cowboy bar, where every night is Saturday night. And it's the closest to a single's bar you're likely to find in Montana. Action around the bars is easy-going, but constant. Partners change about every dance.

The band's first set is given to the over-achievers in country jitterbug. Cowboys and cowgirls swinging and looping and dipping to "Fire on the Mountain," each couple trying to outdo the other. I sit at the bar close to the dance floor on what should be a slow Tuesday night and watch the cowboys' answer to Saturday Night Fever.

Under the barrage of swings, turns, arms under, over, all around their heads and necks, the cowboys' hats never move. And these are good-sized hats. The ten-gallon is back, and many of the cowboys have tucked exotic feathers in their brims. I'm watching the hats and feathers closely, in a growing state of amazement. They are as secure on the cowboys' heads as a Democrat's chances on election night in Butte.

Absolutely everyone is having a good time. Cattle ranchers, having finished business across the street, pull down bourbon ditches and cut into thick tenderloins in the corral of a dining area.

Animated conversations abound. The pool table stays busy. A woman who is 60 if she's a day dances gayly by herself, sometimes joined by a woman friend. All this is tucked neatly into the clear, strong melodies of the band playing all those good old songs — those heart-rending stories of a man and a woman and a few kids trying to make it together.

I'm sitting at the bar close to the dance floor for most of the evening, and I have to laugh when I overhear the conversation of two ranch hands next to me. One guy says to the other, "You know, I was working with this old horse rancher all day, and we went into his house to eat, and he told me to take my hat off. And I said, 'Hell no, I never take my hat off.' And the old guy says in the house he grew up in you always took your hat off. And I said, 'Well, in the house I grew up in we did as we goddamned pleased' . . . . So then I left. I haven't ate yet."

The other guy was sympathetic. "Yeah," he says. "These old guys just don't understand." The hand who hadn't eaten supper got a beer. Through the night he was seen doing a mean jitterbug with several young women. And his hat never moved an inch.

The Lariat

971 Main

Forsyth

Having frequented a home town bar over the years, most of us can cite foibles and heroics of human nature as paraded passed the plank — what would be, if played in fast motion, a telling melodrama of life in the West. Many of them are not featured in this book because their specialness is not obvious to the transient.

So it is difficult for me not to mention my home town's Buffs Bar, Blakesley's, the Oak Room, the Howdy, and a bar now defunct — a favorite in my memory — the Rosebud Lounge.

The Rosebud was underground, under the old drug store. One walked down the steep staircase into a red-lighted den, with dark, mirrored pillars, booths, and the thick, musty smell of the closest thing to decadence I was to experience in my young life in a cow town.

I won't talk of those bars. In other towns I would have passed them by. But there is one Forsyth bar, The Lariat, with a story worth telling.

The story is of a shotgun wedding, a barroom brawl and a subsequent arrest of the bride and groom for disorderly conduct. The young man and woman were married down on the banks of the Yellowstone River east of Forsyth in what must have been a chilly ceremony. It was late December. The groom was escorted to the ceremony by men holding shotguns. They fired the guns into the air when the Justice of the Peace, Alice Wenholz, declared the two man and wife.

Then the wedding party — some 25 people — converged on an unsuspecting downtown Forsyth to celebrate. They began at the Joseph Bar and later moved down the street to the Lariat. It was a wild party. In describing the events of what was to be a long night, the front page story carried in the *Forsyth Independent* noted that some time during the night, the groom was seen in a state of undress dancing with a friend.

The Independent's report of the fight that ensued later in the night is rather confusing, but it went something like this. The fight began when a man made a derogatory remark about the bride, and then pinched her. Two men (neither of them the groom) "stood up for the bride," and the fight was on.

When a woman helping to tend bar tried to stop the fight, she was slugged in the face by one of the men. That brought more men into the fight. The groom and one of the men defending the bride's honor then reportedly hit one of the newcomers to the fight over the head with a pool cue.

The man who hit the woman bartender was ejected from the bar. He broke back through the Lariat's broad plate glass front window to get back into the bar and into the fight, which by this time, was a going brawl.

The police arrived a little after 2 a.m. They found the Lariat's window broken on the sidewalk in front. Broken pool cues, tables, and chairs were scattered throughout the bar. The police called an ambulance for the man who had been clubbed over the head with the pool cue. He had a two-inch cut in his scalp.

Bar owner Joe Kuckler was upset. He pressed charges against the bride and groom and two of their friends. He claimed the groom and the men who defended the bride were the instigators of the fight.

One of the men was charged with disorderly conduct and criminal mischief. The bridegroom was charged with disorderly conduct and released on $100 bail.

Now, here is a couple that will never be at a loss as to what to tell their grandchildren . . . .*

*Paul Harvey picked up the story and related it on his syndicated radio program. I have tried to dig out more background on this tale. I wrote, requesting Harvey's radio transcript, but received no response. The wedding party consisted mainly of newcomers to the area and I've been unable to find an eye witness.

Montana Bar
612 Main Street
Miles City

I wondered when I first walked into the Montana if I had not found a bar about as close to perfect as I was going to find. It was early in my bar search, the weekend of the Bucking Horse Sale in late May. Back to Miles City in the fall — 25 classic bars later — my feelings have not changed.

At first glance the Montana appears the usual down-on-its-luck old-timer's bar. It's name, printed in unwavering gold across the front door, hints of what lies within. In through the heavy glass door, through the entry of leaded glass and old, shining wood, the first impression of tasteful affluence the Montana breaths is found in its fine inlaid terrazzo floor, an intricate pattern of cut green, yellow and white marble.

The back bar is powerful, towering oak, fitted with a brass foot rail and brass spittons. Across from the bar sit beautiful square dark wood booths covered with black horsehide leather. In the center of the stately booths are small oval cherry-wood tables mounted on massive bronze castings that curve with proper neo-Victorian elegance down to the terrazzo marble.

French oak ceiling fans revolve lazily. A finely preserved longhorn steer head, mounted above the booths, stares on the furnishings below. The sun's rays are pleasantly diffused in the pattern of leaded glass as they pour through the expanse of the Montana's front window. A golden light reflects back from the windows, the rich wood, and the smooth, patterned floor.

The Montana was built in 1902 by James Kenney, and outside of a new coat of paint and new wallpaper, the bar has hardly changed. The jukebox and the bar stools are the only modern furnishings. James Kenney never allowed barstools in his bar. You stood at the bar, slung your boot over the brass rail, and drank like a man, or you didn't drink at all.

The booths were meant for business. In the late 1870s the first cattle were driven into Montana from Texas. Miles City was the northernmost point on the route. The Montana was built for those early cattlemen who stayed in Montana and parlayed a bull and a handful of heifers into herds that, when trailed, were about half the size of Connecticut.

Cattlemen, and later the sheepherders — the buyers and the sellers — would meet in the Montana to conduct their business. A back room now used for pool was furnished with chairs and couches, covered like the booths with the black horsehide leather. Reports are that when the men would tire of business, poker or drink, they'd go in the back room and sleep. The Montana was home off the range.

James Kenney's son, George, ran the Montana for years after his father died. It's said he'd put a bottle in front of you and tell you to help yourself. The Montana today isn't exclusively a stockman's bar. But it's changed so little since the old times, it gives the illusion of living its past.

On a weekend like the Bucking Horse Sale, the Montana is a living testimony to the West's lemming-like drive for the Good Time. All of Miles City's bars are packed with raucous, hard-drinkers during the short days and long nights of the Bucking Horse Sale, the town's main annual event.

The **Bison,** next door to the Montana, is well-known as an anything-goes good-timers' bar. The **Trail's End,** across the street from the Montana is the best in the spit-on-the-floor, swing-your-partner bars. Pandemonium reigns in the Trail's End, with complete disregard for life and property giving a wilder tempo to the insane beat of the drunken country western band.

Next door is the **Range Riders,** another classic cowboy bar. The Range Rider's light oak back bar is worth a trip, as well as their dusty and fading black and white photo collection of old-timers and rodeos — shots of bronc riders and ropers when they still held rodeos in ranchers' corrals. There are also a few token photos of sheepmen, a big, old shoeshine stand sitting ready for business, and a fast keno game. A variety of agate jewelry is displayed for sale behind the bar.

The Old Stand
Main Street
Ekalaka

To Montana Ekalaka is the *Town at the End of the Road.* For years the state highway led into the southeastern corner of the state to Ekalaka, but not an inch past. Recently the state paved the road for 18 miles past Ekalaka; then it turns to gravel. But a few more miles of paved road hasn't lessened Ekalaka's reputation as a deadend town. That's why it is ironic that in Montana's early days, the road *started* at Ekalaka.

Around 1888 David Russell, a buffalo hunter and saloon keeper was traveling from the East into Montana with a wagon full of logs that he was going to use to build a saloon. His horses balked in muddy ground. Russell got down from the wagon, spit on the ground, and said, "Hell, any place in Montana is a good place to build a saloon." He threw the logs off the wagon and proceeded to do just that. When he was done, he named it the Old Stand. The town that grew up around Russell's saloon was named for his Ogalala Sioux wife, Igkalaka, (from an Indian word meaning "restless").

The way the crow flies, it's about 80 miles from Forsyth to Ekalaka, a short jaunt in that unpopulated corner of the state. The way the road goes it's a good 150 miles. Ekalakians are an hour from Baker (population about 3,000), a good two hours from Miles City, five hours from a town that could qualify as a city — a town of 1,000 people at best, on the road to nowhere.

A person doesn't just "pass through" Ekalaka, I thought as I sipped my beer, feeling like an outsider at the Old Stand that hot October afternoon. The usual response to "What y'all doin' in Dodge?" — "Just passin' through" — simply would not work in Ekalaka.

Ernie of Ekalaka's Old Stand

In fact, I had the distinct impression that the "just passin' through" response in the Old Stand would bring on gales of wild laughter. I had gone a total of 300 miles out of my way to be in the Old Stand sipping beer. Passing through, indeed.

The bartender doesn't know quite what to do with me. I'm the only woman in the bar — and a young, unattached stranger at that. Finally he saunters over and we talk a little about the end of the road. "Yeah," he says, "we get left out of a lot of things. Maybe it's for the best. You don't get bothered by a lot of outsiders."

He tells me the original Old Stand built by Russell was torn down a few years ago. This Old Stand was built around 1902 and remodeled in 1953. Several feet across from the bar are old padded vinyl booths. The space in between is used for dancing on busy nights. In the back, to the side, is another large room used for dances and receptions. There's a cafe connected to the bar. The only picture on the wall is an old one of Abraham Lincoln.

It's mid-afternoon and the Old Stand is beginning to fill. A few old cowboys gather at the end of the long bar; on the other end young men take a break from construction work. One good-looking, brown-eyed young man says to another, "Hey, why don't you bring the old lady down. I need somebody to dance with." Silence for a moment. "No one will dance with me," the guy continues. Another pause. Finally the other guy says, "Hell, they all know ya."

The old cowboys sit at the end of the long bar, greeting each other cordially when they meet. They drink beer only from a glass, but roll their own cigarettes.

Interest perks when I get the camera out and begin to shoot a few frames of the bar and the old cowboys. In other towns a camera can kill all possibilities of a good conversation with people. In Ekalaka, it's an opening. A couple of the men at the bar tell me to talk to Ernie, one of the old guys at the end of the bar. Ernie hears and sits up a little closer to the bar for the picture.

Ernie is a convivial, weather-beaten, barrel-chested, throaty old man. A worn black Stetson pushed to the back of his head frames a face at one minute dead-pan serious, the next breaking into jigsaw puzzle lines with his cigarette hack of a laugh.

A crowd gathers around to egg Ernie on. "Tell her the sister-in-law story," one guy says. Chuckles from the group. "Ah, naw," says Ernie, "not that one."

"All right, then tell her about stealing the horses." Ernie served a little time after he was caught trucking another man's horses from some point in South Dakota. Getting caught didn't bother him much, according to Ernie. Just another day's work. I ask him why he did it. The answer is something like, "because they were there."

Then there's the story about how the cattle rustlers would butcher their take and throw the head and hooves down a well; how he burnt down the bar of a guy who was his only competition in Alzada; how he once sold a dude 12 quarts of Black Roses (a whisky brewed from potatoes) claiming it was the best he had, and charging accordingly.

This Ernie is quite the scoundrel. But they keep asking for the sister-in-law story, and that is the one Ernie won't tell. Ernie tells me he's been married nine times if you don't count the weddings on the reservation. "I couldn't keep a woman," Ernie says. "I'd usually get 'em in the fall and lose 'em in the spring. Then I'd have to get another one."

A few of the guys won't buy it that Ernie's been married only nine times. Ernie's only child from all those unions runs the Old Stand. Ernie's son passes, and a guy says, "Hey, Sam, how many times' Ernie been married?"

"Nine," Ernie reiterates. "Hell," says Sam, "you've been married 12 or 13 times." Gales of laughter from the crowd. Tell her the sister-in-law story. Naw, says Ernie, not that one.

"You ought to stay for the wedding dance," Ernie tells me. "It'll be a good one." As I was driving to Ekalaka the Baker radio station had announced several times a wedding dance for Zane and Barb Saturday night in the Old Stand. Everyone within the radio's wave pattern is invited. Ernie and the boys are keenly anticipating it. They all try to talk me into staying the night (it's Friday) and being around for the dance.

I've had several beers bought for me by this time, and staying overnight is tempting. A wedding dance in Ekalaka would be an occasion that would live on in memory. And who can say when I'll be in Ekalaka again? Being in Ekalaka, to me, is still something like being in another country. It's removal alone makes it precious. Naw, I have to go, I say, they're expecting me back in Forsyth.

Ernie's ninth wife comes in. A pleasant middle-aged woman, she is a nursing student in Miles City and commutes to Ekalaka on weekends. Ernie transforms from the rollicking scoundrel to the righteous, gentle husband. He invites me to stay at their place overnight. It's hard to say no. I gather my things and start for the door.

As I leave, the man who had led the laughter is the fourth person to say to me — in these same words — "Sure hate to see ya go."

Sure hate to see ya go. Words out of a time when Montanans were fewer, when a stranger became a friend in a few hours and a neighbor closer than kin in a matter of days.

The Jersey Lilly
Ingomar

Ingomar, at one time, was the largest sheep-shearing town in the world if you listen to Bill Seward of the Jersey Lilly. In the very early days—before fences divided the land—Bill says they'd trail sheep east from a good part of central Montana (White Sulphur Springs, Two Dot, Big Timber) and shear them in Ingomar. Then they'd push the woolies on to Glendive where they were sent East to a market of immigrants who still preferred mutton to beef.

The sheep men chose Ingomar as the gathering and shearing place because the land around it had less hills and coulees than other routes. Chances of keeping the herd together were better through Ingomar. When sheep did stray they were easy to locate.

The Milwaukee railroad had big plans for Ingomar as a sheep-shipping center at one time, too. But Seward says the homesteaders eventually crowded the big sheep men out. And so Ingomar, once a wool man's boom town, now seems deserted until you reach the end of a dusty road — main street Ingomar — and see the proud sign of the Jersey Lilly.

The wood-planked porch and hitching post haven't changed much in the decades they've been around. The Jersey Lilly rises from them — a sturdy yellow brick (once the town bank), and stands weather-beaten, dust-ridden, age-worn, but unrelenting — a stalwart to the weather-beaten, dust-ridden sheep and cattle men she still serves.

The Jersey Lilly is one of two or three bars in a radius of at least 40 miles of dry, windblown alkali-white plains between Forsyth and Roundup on Highway 12. Just looking over the land on a warm day will bring on the thirst of a man nine days into hell. So the Jersey Lil is more precious than many bars. But there's more to the Lil than liquid refreshment.

Bill Seward serves four cuts of steak, sandwiches, his famous beans cooked in a mildly hot, thin broth, delicately sliced orange and onion that he insists you pile on a saltine cracker and eat in one bite. (The combination is surprisingly good.) He sells a wide range of staples, postcards, general merchandise, and pumps gas on the side. He opens at 7 a.m. and closes when no one has come in for a spell.

The Jersey Lilly has one of the older back bars I've found — a small, ornate cherry wood. The ceiling is a fine old pressed tin painted a rich cream white. The floor is worn wood planks. Small tables draped with cotton cloths sit opposite the bar. The kitchen is open and off to the side. In front of it are shelves stocked with groceries. In the back there's a pool table and a room sometimes used for dances. There is no television set in the Jersey Lilly, and there never will be as long as Bill Seward is tending bar. "People come here to drink . . ." he tells me.

The Jersey Lilly serves as a gathering place for the people spread thinly over the prairie, but Seward's fine home cooking and the old-time character of the place bring in folks who drive miles out of their way for a drink, a steak, a bowl of beans, or just a chat with the Seward's. I know people who live in Miles City who will call from Billings to tell Bill to take a couple of tenderloins out of the freezer—they're coming through. They'll reroute through Ingomar, a good 60 miles out of their way.

Another common practice among certain groups is to organize a party, call Bill to tell him how many steaks to take out of the freezer, and then head for Ingomar. "People come here and make their own fun," Bill says.

Part of the allure is that the Jersey Lil is old and tough. The Jersey Lil is so old and tough it has no inside John. You still

have to walk out the back door to the outhouses. But like about everything else in Ingomar, there's more to that story than meets the eye.

Ingomar never has had its own water. There's no aquifer within drilling distance, no chance of well water anywhere near Ingomar. Since the beginning, water has been brought in on the Milwaukee rail, 2,000 gallons for $12, delivered every couple of days. That's a real steal for Ingomar considering what the town faces should the bankrupt Milwaukee quit running, as it is threatening. To truck water from Melstone, a town slightly larger than Ingomar about 20 miles down the road, Ingomar would pay a cent and a half a gallon, or nearly three times what is paid the railroad.

So it's easy to understand why Ingomar has never enjoyed the luxury of modern man's flush toilets. I don't know if they would put in flush toilets at the Jersey Lil if fresh water began gurgling from the earth. I'd bet on the continuation of the outhouses. Bill tells me the state authorities made them put flush toilets in their little schoolhouse in Ingomar — the only ones in town. He was just a little disgusted. "It's pretty darned expensive for that much water," he says, adding he went to school without flush toilets and he learned just as much as the kids are learning today.

About 30 people live in Ingomar. The town has stayed at that population for years. Shortly after World War II, there were no bars open in Ingomar. They'd closed when so many of the area's young men had gone to war. Bill's father sent his daughter up to the town store to get a pack of cigarettes one evening. She came back empty-handed, saying the store had closed. Bill's dad said, "By golly, when you can't get a pack of cigarettes or a drink in a town at nine o'clock, you'd better do something about it." So he opened the Jersey Lilly in the old bank building, naming it for the famed combination bar/courtroom of Texan hanging Judge Roy Bean.

Bill, his wife Martha, and his brother, Les, share shifts at the Lilly. The afternoon I'm there is the day before antelope season opens. Bill is making bucks right and left on the hunters. Pumping gas, selling supplies, drinks, food.

One group comes in for his beans. Bill serves them up in large bowls and leaves a hot kettle on the table should they want more. He mumbles to me as he heads back to the kitchen, "Some days I go through 20 gallons of these beans." I'm eating a sweet, juicy T-bone, slices of onion and orange on saltine crackers, drinking a beer. The world's looking good from my vantage point at the Jersey Lil.

The Highline

Oxford Bar & Billiard Parlor

331 First Street

Havre

The gusty December day I blow into Havre many men are standing near the end of the Oxford's long bar. I take a seat at the front. It takes a while for the bartender to notice me, sitting way up front. After she's noticed me, she's still in no rush to serve me. A look around tells me I'm sitting at a fountain. It's the kind of fountain used in pharmacies and ice cream parlors, a remnant of speak-easy days. It has the stainless steel coke holders, the pointed paper cups, the oval stainless steel doors opening into the ice cream cooler, the old Hamilton blenders. The bar plank connects to the fountain — a handsome grey Italian marble — and together they extend the length of the room.

The marble is beautiful, fine and smooth to the touch. The coke stands bring on happy memories of childhood. It's nice to be out of the wind. But it's beer I came in for. It occurs to me the most potent libation I may be served at the fountain may be an extra-thick chocolate malt. Finally I get the bartender's attention. I ask if she serves beer at this end of the bar. "If ya want a beer," she says, her eyes mean, "you can have a beer."

So I have a beer, by gosh.

I wasn't too far off about the chocolate malt. The Oxford's fountain still does a spritely milkshake business. More than that, it functions as a select mercantile for its customers. Many objects are for sale: shoestrings, Vick's inhalers, cigarette lighters, Anacin, Coffee Nips, Bromo Seltzer dispensed in one-shot quantities from a suspended bottle, hot dogs, liverwurst sandwiches, coffee, fifteen cents a cup.

The Oxford would be a good-looking bar if it weren't cluttered with miscellany. It has one of the nicer pressed tin ceilings I've found, and what seem to be the original globe lights. A beautiful marble back bar that matches the fountain sits to the front, but it is nearly covered by shelves holding one-shot bottles of liquor. Above the fountain bar is an elaborately rigged up table supported on one side by the bar and held on the other by a suspended chain. On it sits a massive console television set in an ugly wood cabinet. I never saw the television on. To the side is a poker pit and a lively afternoon game.

The Oxford is a tough bar. You have to get a key to go to the ladies' room. However, a sign on the front door says it is closed Sundays. Now what kind of a tough bar would close on Sundays?

I suppose a bar owned by Chuck Colier. Chuck is a happy guy, a family man, congenial as a Miss America contestant. After a short conversation with him you understand why he closes on Sundays, but not why he keeps the ladies' room locked. He talks with an energy most people couldn't summon under a fire alert, a surprising energy considering he has spent his entire working life in one place — the Oxford Beer Parlor.

Chuck began at the Oxford as a shoeshine boy in the 1930s. By the time the bar came up for sale in 1958 Chuck had shined hundreds of shoes, blended thousands of milkshakes, pushed a broom countless still-dark mornings, and tended bar, too. He said he'd been there so long he thought he might as well buy it. The shoeshine stand he once used sits opposite the fountain, a once opulent three-chair amazon of a shoeshine stand, now a decrepit white elephant, seldom if ever used. Now his daughter, Cynthia, is sharing shifts with him at the Oxford.

Chuck remembers working at the Oxford fountain during Prohibition days. He claims he sold from 60 to 100 milkshakes a night. He also remembers Ma Plaz, Havre's black matriarch. Ma Plaz dates back to Fort Assiniboine days. She operated a house of ill repute near the Fort. When the Fort closed in 1907 she moved into Havre and opened a tiny cafe.

She commanded considerable respect in Havre. Chuck remembers when he worked the fountain one of the first instructions he received from his boss was that an old colored lady would be coming in and when she did to be sure to give her a cigar. Sure enough, every afternoon in would come Ma Plaz, and every afternoon Chuck would promptly give her her cigar.

Ma Plaz made the rounds to many saloons in Havre daily. When Prohibition lifted she'd get a drink in every bar, as well as a cigar, if that was what she wanted.

Chuck is full of good stories, but the late afternoon is bringing in a crowd. A guy hollers from the poker table, "One swing, Chuck," and Chuck is gone. I soon realize one swing is what usually is called a round. I decide I like the term. I think of Ma Plaz and her method of "swinging" through Havre.

The Palace Bar
228 First Street
Havre

I'm talking with Ward Compton, former owner of the Palace Bar in Havre. Ward is a pleasant, articulate man who looks like he could be a bank officer or a wealthy rancher. He's telling me, "All I've ever done is follow a cow around or have a saloon."

The handsome Native American sitting next to me adds an amen: "That's what you call a Montanan." He touches his chin to his neck in a deep nod.

Ward's owned several bars across the state — the Loring bar, the Oasis in Manhattan, a bar in Fort Benton, and of course, the Palace. He ran the Palace for 17 years before selling it to his son, Jupe, a few years ago. Ward still spends a good deal of time in the bar, most of it in supervising the poker game in the back.

"Everybody, regardless of who they are or what they do, should spend a little time bartending," Ward says. "You mingle with the bums, the people who are average and the aristocrats — it's a hell of an experience. You meet a lot of people in all states of mind."

Ward leaves to start the poker game, and the Indian to my left, a mixed blood he says — quite a mix, too, Irish, French,

Assiniboine and Chippewa Cree — is telling me that all kinds of people frequent the Palace. "They don't frown on minorities here," he says. "This is the best bar in Havre."

Later Ward is to add his amen to that. "There's an awful lot of good Indians now days," he tells me. The night I'm in, an Indian approaches the bar with a check he wants cashed. Ward looks at it — sees it's for about $400 — gives it to the man to endorse and then counts out the money. Most of the good old-time bars still serve as a bank for their regular customers.

The Palace also serves as a seasonal employment service for select customers. Farmers and ranchers will come to the Palace when they need workers, Ward tells me. Havre, with its freight connections and seasonal farm work, is on the migrant workers' route. Many migrants will make the Palace their first stop when they arrive in Havre. Jupe is hospitable. He puts their packs behind the bar while they look around town.

When a farmer or rancher comes in looking for help, Jupe or Ward match employer with employee. Ward claims many farmers and ranchers would rather hire a man out of a bar than a man who refrains from drink, but relies on government or local assistance. "They think they can get a better quality man out of a bar," Ward says.

The Palace has a majestic mahogany back bar — a back bar resembling the Turf's that burned down in Missoula, the Club Cigar in Great Falls, and the New Atlas in Columbus — a style of back bar that is becoming a pattern in my search.

The next day I spend a little time with Ward. He has a few good stories. One is about a guy and his dream of winning big in Las Vegas. "There was this guy, and the height of his ambition was to go to Nevada. He saved his money and bought a car and went to Las Vegas. He showed up back in Havre in two weeks. He'd lost everything. He came in here and told us, 'They treated me real good in Las Vegas. I went down there in a $3,000 car and came back in a $20,000 bus.'"

Another gambler story: "We used to gamble when it was illegal," Ward tells me. "The law was always pretty good if you kept it in reason. When the police got too tough I had a room in the basement. We had a poker game that had gone on for 20 hours. An old man — Martin Wolfe — he was about 70 years old — finally dozed off to sleep at the table.

"Martin was a gambler and that was it — a *good* gambler. It's real dark down there in the basement — no windows or anything. We turned the lights off and then dealt the cards,

The Palace

pretending we were playing. It was pitch black. Martin woke up when we were bidding and started feeling around.

" 'You guys gotta help me,' he said. We just kept on like we were playing. Martin got more upset. He really thought he was in trouble. We kept playing. 'By God, Ward,' he said, 'I'm not joshing, I'm plumb blind' . . . ."

Before my trip I had been told to see a man named Shorty Young who had a saloon in Havre. I asked around a few bars. No one seemed to recognize the name and I thought I might have the wrong town.

Finally Chuck Colier at the Oxford told me Shorty had been dead for years. But he did have quite a saloon — the Chain of Lakes — three riotous floors. There were bars on two floors, with gambling and a crib row on one and an auditorium with a live show on another. Chuck tells me the entertainment usually was girlie shows. Around war time, he remembers, the girls would dance nude behind an American flag.

Yeah, Shorty was quite a guy, Ward Compton tells me later. He donated to every church and community organization around. Because he was such a righteous man — outside of his business — the law usually looked the other way.

"When he died," Ward says, "they padlocked the door. The bar was never opened again."

About The Highline

Before my trip to the highline I hadn't been able to identify many choice saloons in that vast stretch of land forming the northeastern corner of the state. I was confident once I was able to do a little firsthand research a whole new world of saloon life would open to me. But if there was a new world up there, my boat missed the shore.

A five-day loop through Malta and Glasgow, on to Wolf Point and Scobey and Plentywood, then down through Circle, Sidney and Glendive did little to inspire my search. The locals couldn't name any bars of note.

The old saloons had either been renovated beyond recognition or no longer existed. So, as I traveled those 1,500 miles in that eerie meditation of land and sky I developed a theory.

The highline was settled by farmers — family men, for the most part — unlike the cowboys and rustlers to the south, the gold panners to the southwest and the trappers in the northwest. The sodbusters were more likely to put up a church than another saloon.* The towns they built during the boom farming years of the early 1900s were left to the relentless drought wind of 1917-19 that swept the state, carrying with it a mass exodus of bankrupt honyockers. If there were few saloons to begin with, you can be sure few survived the killing drought and more than a decade of Prohibition.

It is a little ironic that the nomadic cultures of the cowboy,

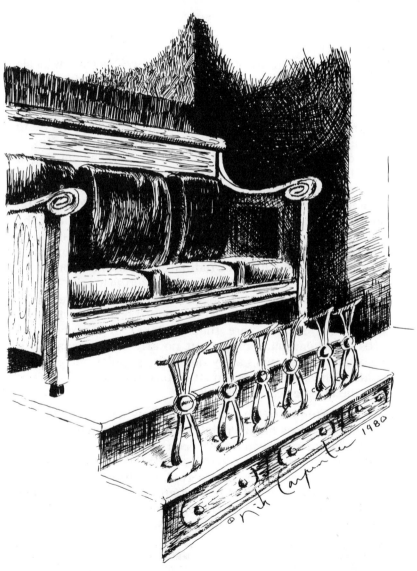

Shoeshine Stand at the Oxford

the miner and the trapper, as reflected in their saloons, would have more permanence than that of the honyocker. But it is easy to understand when one remembers the social importance of the saloon to the drifter in unsettled territory.

There obviously is a saloon life on the highline, whether or not I found any noteworthy saloons. One of the more interesting towns for bars is Plentywood. Here we see the mercenary commerce of a border town on the right side of the buck. At the time of my visit the Canadian dollar was worth about eighty-five cents. Bob Nielsen of **Bob & Lou's Place** tells me that even with the fifteen cent loss on the dollar, the Canadians find the lower price of U.S. goods and services worth a trip south.

To serve this influx of Canadians, as well as the few locals around, Plentywood has developed its own breed of saloon — ultra-modern, all-purpose and huge. The two main such monsters are the **Blue Moon** and the **Golden Wheel,** both on Highway 16 south of town. It seems the idea is to hold on to customers by providing all the vital services in one building — food, drink, dancing and entertainment — to say nothing of gambling, which is something folks in Plentywood try to say nothing about.

The day I'm in town I spend some time in Bob & Lou's (105 South Main). Although not as large as the Blue Moon or the Golden Wheel, Bob and Lou's has the same appeal. Besides the bar, there's a large dining area, a disco in the back (probably the only disco in a 200-mile radius) and two large rooms on a lower floor suited out entirely for what Bob slyly calls "cards."

The Golden Wheel and the **Spot Bar** (across the street from Bob & Lou's) had been raided the month before my visit. FBI agents had seized more than $18,000 in currency and $10,000 in gambling chips, but no arrests were made. An Associated Press news story noted the popular game in the Golden Wheel was Canadian stuke poker, which Bob Nielsen tells me is American blackjack.

I'm talking with Bob, who only smiles when I ask what kind of gambling goes on downstairs. I'm getting nowhere until a big Canadian who would have been very mean had he been a little less drunk comes into the bar. He heads straight for the card rooms. Finding them deserted, he stumbles back up to the bar and demands to know where the stuke game is. Bob smiles, but says nothing. In Plentywood it's okay to smile, but when they ask about the stuke games, it's best to say nothing.

*K. Ross Toole provides an interesting view of the life of the sodbuster in *Twentieth Century Montana: A State of Extremes.* He writes: "It was a rare honyocker who drank or gambled. These towns were not created for diversion but for cold, hard utility — granary, general store, bank, and church . . . ."